D0216227

DATE DUE

DEMCO 38-296

MATHEMATICS

FOR

COSMETOLOGY

by

MARGARET B. FLECK

Teacher of Cosmetology
Revised by
Jacob J. Yahm

Milady Publishing Company
(A Division of Delmar Publishers, Inc.)
Tarrytown, NY 10591

Riverside Community College
Library
4800 Magnolia Avenue
Riverside, California 92506

TT958 .F4 1982
Fleck, Margaret B.
Mathematics for cosmetology

1990 Printing
© Copyright 1954-1966-1975-1982
Milady Publishing Company
(A Division of Delmar Publishers, Inc.)
Tarrytown, N.Y.

ISBN 0-87350-128-4
Library of Congress Card No. 75-24818
All Rights Reserved

Reproduction or translation of any part of this work beyond that permitted by
sections 107 and 108 of the 1976 United States Copyright Act without
permission of the copyright owner is unlawful. Requests for permission and
further information should be addressed to the Permissions Department,
Milady Publishing Company.

Printed in the United States of America

10 9 8 7 6 5 4 3 2 1

PREFACE

Cosmetology and its allied branches make up one of the leading businesses in this country. To operate successfully in this industry, it is important for participants to know something about the mathematics connected with it.

Not only must beauty salon owners be proficient in their work, they must also be good business people. Many salon owners, while being artists, have failed in business because they lacked the mathematical training to figure costs, service prices, and losses or profits. To operate a beauty salon successfully, the owner or manager must know how to figure the cost of operation by the month, day and hour, in order to determine how much to charge for the various services performed in the salon, what salaries to pay, which employees are making a profit on their work, the cost of supplies, and many other items.

This short review of elementary mathematics is designed to refresh the memory of those who may need it. The student should master the contents of this book before attempting to solve the problems pertaining to the successful operation of a beauty salon.

Mathematics should be a "must" in training students for successful careers in the practice of cosmetology. Every practicing cosmetologist, regardless of how long ago he or she has completed the training program, can profit materially from it.

This short program in mathematics is a review of basic arithmetic, and includes problems encountered in conducting a successful beauty salon.

Why Study Mathematics

Cosmetology students should be aware of the problems presented here because:

1. They should know how to solve the problems successfully if and when they start in business for themselves.

2. By becoming acquainted with these problems while still in their training, they will better understand the expenses involved in running a salon, and why certain financial decisions are made by the salon owner.

Cosmetologists should remember that there are other expenses connected with the operation of a beauty salon besides salaries and rent. It is hoped that through this program students will become aware of the importance of using time and supplies to their best advantage, thus benefitting themselves and their employers.

Study Hints

These are a few guides students can follow when solving problems:

1. Read the problem carefully as many times as is necessary in order to understand what is being asked for.

2. Determine which given facts will help in solving the problems.

3. Decide if the solution of the problem requires addition, subtraction, multiplication, division, or all of these.

4. Solve the problem and decide whether or not the answer sounds reasonable.

5. Check the answer by working the problem backwards, if possible. Students are advised to be neat and systematic in this mathematics program, as well as in all other cosmetology training. Every figure and decimal point must be plainly written. The answer and other important parts of each problem should be labeled.

All arithmetical exercises or problems involve the use of one or more of four possible processes: namely, addition, subtraction, multiplication and division. Skill in performing these fundamental processes accurately and with reasonable speed depends upon diligent, correct practice.

CONTENTS

ADDITION

The process of combining two or more numbers and expressing the result as a single number is called *addition*.

Each number is called an *addend*, and the result is called the *sum*.

Example: #1 Add:

            6438 - addend
            4957 - addend
           ─────
           11395 - sum

#2   5324)
      482)
      249)   addends
     6392)
     4653)
    ──────
    17100   sum

Checking answer achieved by addition.

Method One:
   Add the columns of figures from top to bottom, then add them from bottom to top.

Method Two:
   Add each column separately and arrange the totals as illustrated:

225	First Column Total 18
350	Second Column Total 23
786	Third Column Total 27
666	2948
921	
2948	

Method Three:
   Check by the elimination of 9's. This method is illustrated in the following problem:

Example:

369,424	(369,424)	=	424	=	10	=	1	(1)
78,916	(78,916)	=	76	=	13	=	4	(4)
29,043	(29,043)	=	0	=	0	=	0	(0)
5,125	(5,125)	=	5125	=	13	=	4	(4)
68,432	(68,432)	=	842	=	14	=	5	(5)
								5
550,940	(550,940)	=		5				

EXPLANATION:
   Eliminate the 9's or any combination of digits that add up to 9, in the first addend by crossing out the 3 and the 6, then the 9. This leaves the digit 424; add these numbers and you get 10. Add 1 + 0 = 1. Repeat this process for the other addends. Eliminate the 9's or any combination of digits that add up to 9 from the remainders; then add, and your answer is 5. Then do the same for the sum of the addition. Here your remainder is 5, thus proving the answer is correct. If you received a different number other than 5, then your answer would be incorrect and you would have to add the digits again.

Exercise I

Show proof of the total to each of the following problems:

1	2	3	4	5	6
9	11	76	12	69	7.85
7	19	34	32	58	19.26
8	16	23	68	47	59.79
9	15	89	18	93	.66
			74	25	7.40
				36	

7	8	9	10	11	12
756	696	671	59	821	671
172	694	112	80	372	112
934	821	856	77	694	856
514	372	1291	35	453	291
283	575	65	49	575	65
	453	140	93	696	140
		668			668

13	14	15	16
$9225.45	$846.79	$56.27	$63.48
$6005.34	130.45	32.46	21.16
9870.02	68.04	187.92	80.20
2256.73	9.56	223.18	83.05
9875.64	30.47	65.75	90.66
		74.46	

17	18	19	20
308,625	10,481,898	2,431,782	3,069
159,087	251,569	1,001,576	31,283
868,510	884,423	17,031	507,544
215,763	14,210,652	254,973	84,986
	3,091,567	771,290	255,900
		963	1,409,355

Exercise II

Example:

Copy 47	47
Add 93	93
Below second row write sum of line 1 and 2	140
	233
Below third line write sum of line 2 and 3	373
	606
Continue until there are 8 lines.	979
Add columns. Prove the answer	1585
	4056

Add the following as illustrated above:

1	2	3	4	5	6
9	11	76	14	11	75
7	19	34	23	44	70

7	8	9	10	11	12	13
55	58	41	85	28	24	50
55	84	49	95	31	92	98

14	15	16	17	18	19	20
86	53	625	756	683	4786	3755
66	70	624	998	749	1411	6099

Problems in Addition

1. Miss Jones' daily services amounted to the following: Tues. $52.50, Wed. $52.30, Thurs. $71.20, Fri. $76.80, Sat. $90.80. How much did Miss Jones take in for services for the week?

   _____

2. Miss Adams rendered services amounting to the following: Tues. $55.75, Wed. $51.00, Thurs. $60.25, Fri. $76.50, and Sat. $84.75. Find the total amount for her services for the week.

   _____

3. Miss Brown's services amounted to the following: Tues, $57.25, Wed. $69.75, Thurs. $79.00, Fri. $75.00 and Sat. $90.00. Find the weekly total.

   _____

4. Miss Adams sold the following cosmetics in March: 1st week $21.10, 2nd week $11.85, 3rd week $30.80, 4th week $32.00. Find the monthly total.

   _____

5. Miss Smith's services for the day were: hair lightening $30.00, brow arch $10.00, Hair shapings $15.00, scalp treatments $10.00, shampoos & sets $35.00. Find the total amount.

   _____

6. Miss Smith performed services and sales as follows: Shampoos and sets $35.00, hair tints $15.00, hair lightening $30.00, hair shapings $15.00, sales face powder $5.00, combs $4.00, scalp ointments $6.00. Find the total amount.

   _____

7. Miss Mead made the following cash payments: window cleaner $18.00, express $9.35, merchandise for resale $46.40, cleaning supplies $9.30, hair tints $43.15, permanent wave solutions $31.00. How much money did she pay out?

   _____

8. Miss Mead wrote checks for the following items: rent $300.00, electricity $53.00, equipment $78.75, supplies $86.15, sales tax $43.10. How much was paid by checks?

   _____

9. Miss Mead made the following payments: Miss Jones' salary $150.75, Miss Smith's salary $125.10, Miss Adams' salary $129.18, Miss Brown's salary $150.25, and drew out $180.00 for her personal use. How much was paid out?

_____

SUBTRACTION

The process of finding the excess of one number over another is called *subtraction*.
The number from which we subtract is called the *minuend*, and the number subtracted, the *subtrahend*.

The result or difference obtained is called the *difference* or *remainder*.

Examples

Example #1: Subtract:

      749 - minuend   #2:   57243 - minuend

      363 - subtrahend   31964 - subtrahend

      386 - difference (remainder)   25279 - difference (remainder)

Prove the answers in subtraction by adding the difference (remainder) to the subtrahend (quantity subtracted). The resulting number should be the minuend, the quantity from which the subtraction was made.

Examples

Example #1:   749   #2:   57243

             −363) add   −31964) add

             386)   25279)

             749   minuend   57243   minuend

Exercise III

Subtract the following: ———— Prove your answers.

1	2	3	4
54	152	395	14.7
−49	−56	−278	−7.3

5	6	7	8
9.071	46.97	.07	8.
−5.6	−26.08	−.068	−5.667

9	10	11	12
76.5	970.1	80.203	47,502
−41.0	−497.9	−41.866	−35,788

13	14	15
805,002	3,609.072	6,007.140
−396,987	−2,098.649	−3,998.387

16	17	18
816,480	638,467	200.1
−271,842	−347,579	− 19.782

19	20
369.01	670.34
− 49.7896	− 1.09002

MAKING CHANGE

When giving change to a patron the "Austrian Method" is generally used. Instead of subtracting the amount owed from the coin or bill given, the amount of the purchase is added to the next higher money unit, then to the next and so on until the amount of the coin or bill is reached.

For example, if a patron's check amounts to $2.20 and she gives a $5.00 bill in payment, the cashier should say, "$2.20 out of $5.00," and place the bill on the ledge of the cash register under the keys. (The transaction should be completed before the bill is placed in the cash drawer. This avoids confusion in case of any question.)

The cashier gives the following in making the change: 5 cents to make the sum of $2.25; then 25 cents to make $2.50; 50 cents to make $3.00; then 2 one dollar bills to complete the total of $5.00.

Problems

1. Miss Adams presented her patron with a check listing the following services: shampoo and set, $15.00; oil manicure, $5.25; and a hand and arm massage, $3.50.

   a) Find the total amount of the bill.
   b) The patron pays with a $50.00 bill. Using the "Austrian Method" explain how Miss Adams makes the change.

   c) How much does the patron receive from her $50.00?

a) _____   b) _____   c) _____

2. A patron bought 1 jar of cleansing cream for $3.75, 1 jar tissue cream $4.25, 1 box face powder $3.75, 1 lipstick $2.75.

   a) What is the total amount of the bill?
   b) She paid with a $20 bill. What change did the patron receive?
   c) How should the change be counted?

a) _____   b) _____   c) _____

3. Miss Mead presented her patron with a check listing the following: permanent wave $35.50; manicure $5.25; haircut $15.50; facial $15.25.

   a) What is the total amount? _____

   b) The patron paid with one $50.00 bill and three $10.00 bills. What change did she receive?_____

   c) How should the change be counted? _____

4. Miss Mead paid $56.85 for an order of cosmetics. She made a profit of $28.74 on the order.

   a) How much did she receive for the cosmetics?_____

   b) She paid for the order with a $100.00 bill.
      How much change did she receive?_____

   c) Count out the change she received. _____

5. Mrs. Green had a manicure $5.50; a shampoo and set $15.50 and a hair shaping $15.50.

   a) What would be her total bill if she treated her sister also to
      the same service? _____

   b) Mrs. Green paid the bill with four $20.00 bills.
      How much change did she receive? _____

   c) How should it be counted out? _____

6. Mrs. French had a shampoo and set the price of which was $15.50. She also had a manicure $5.25 and a brow arch $9.50.

   a) How much change did she receive from two $20.00 bills? _____

   b) Responding to a special sale, she then decided to buy lipstick $1.75, face powder $2.75 and skin lotion $1.85. How much is her bill? _____

   c) What is her change from a $10.00 bill? _____

7. Miss Jones had services amounting to $6.75. She bought a box of face powder $2.20, a lip brush $.95, a brow brush $.65 and a jar of cleansing cream $3.40.
   a) What is the total of her bill? _____

   b) Count out her change from a $20.00 bill. _____

MULTIPLICATION

Multiplication is, in reality, abbreviated addition. It is the process by which one number is added to itself as many times as there are units in another number.

Example:

4 × 6 means "4 added to itself 6 times,"
$$4 + 4 + 4 + 4 + 4 + 4 = 24$$
or
6 × 4 means "6 added to itself 4 times,"
$$6 + 6 + 6 + 6 = 24$$

The number to be added a certain number of times is called the *multiplicand*, and the number of times it is to be added is called the *multiplier*. The result of all this addition is called the *product*.

```
Multiply          732 — multiplicand
      (by)  ×      36 — multiplier
                 4392
                 2196
                26352 — product
```

Checks or Proof for Multiplication

Method One:

Divide the product by the multiplier, and if the quotient is the same as the multiplicand, the multiplication is correct.

Method Two:

Use the same method used in checking addition by eliminating 9's.

Example:

```
 3849 ---------- 24      ----------     6
 × 23 ----------  5      ----------     5
11547                                  30  -----  3
 7698
88527 ---------- 30      ----------     3
```

Exercise IV

Multiply and prove the following:

1	2	3	4	5
415	895	578	835	396,750
× 6	× 9	× 11	× 78	× 43

6	7	8	9
6843	578	$9.76	765004
× 88	× 13	× 75	× 864

10	11	12	13
$96.58	8731	22186	961432
× 407	× 563	× 4224	× 79

14	15	16	17
9999	92.83	530.72	552.69
× 709	× 7.89	× 3072	× 621

18	19	20
$456.48	$15867	5068514
× 48	× 738	× 4001

Problems

1. Miss Mead bought the following merchandise to replenish her stock: 1 doz. boxes face powder at $2.29 each, 1 doz. lipstick at $1.95 each, 1½ doz. skin refresher at $1.45 each.

   What is the total amount of the bill? _____

2. Miss Henry worked part time as follows: Tuesday and Wednesday, 7 hrs. each, Thursday 5 hrs., Friday 6 hrs. and Saturday 4½ hrs. She was paid $3.90 per hour.

   a) How much did she earn in salary?
   b) She also received the following tips: Tues. $10.00, Wed. $10.75, Thurs. $15.50, Fri. and Sat. $25.00 each. What is the total amount she received for the week?

   a) _____   b) _____

3. A cosmetologist must *double* her salary before the employer can realize any profit from her work.

   Miss Mead paid Miss Adams $125.00 per week to start. The first week Miss Adams' services amounted to $162.00. How much did Miss Mead lose on the first week's work? _____

4. Miss Dodd's salary is $125.00 per week. In the first week her intake for services amounted to $97.00, 2nd week $105.00, 3rd week, $112.00, 4th week $135.00, 5th week $120.00 (Conditions on salary as stated in Problem 3.)

   How much did her employer lose on salary paid to Miss Dodd in the first 5 weeks of work? _____

5. Miss Mead pays Miss Brown $125.00 per week. How much money must she take in for services if Miss Mead is to realize $50.00 profit on her work? (Conditions on salary the same as in Problem 3.) _____

11

6. The cost of cold permanent wave solution per permanent is $4.25, shampoo $.20, 3 towels at $.17 each to launder, 2½ hours of cosmetologist's time at $3.90 per hour, retention papers $.09 and overhead costs including heat, light, rent, etc. $5.63.

   a) What is the actual cost of the permanent wave?

   b) What is the profit if the permanent wave is priced at $35.00?

   a) _____   b) _____

7. Mrs. Jones bought the following for her beauty salon:
   6 jars hand cream @ $1.95 per jar
   7 jars emollient cream @ $3.20 per jar
   8 jars cleansing cream @ $2.75 per jar
   1 qt. astringent @ $3.95 per quart

   What is the total amount of her bill? _____

8. Figure the cost of a newspaper ad for a beauty salon that is one column 7 inches at $5.25 per inch.

   Note: Newspaper advertising is sold by inches per column. *Example:* One column 3 inches means taking the space of one column 3 inches long. If the cost was $5.25 per inch the one column 3 inches would be 3 inches $\times$ $5.25 or $15.75 for the ad.

9. Mr. Gerard opened a new beauty salon. He took a large ad which measured 3 columns 10 inches. How much did he pay for the ad at the rate of $5.25 one column inch? _____

10. The average newspaper has 8 columns and the printed space is 22 inches long. At $5.45 per column inch, what would be the cost of a half page ad? _____

DIVISION

The process of finding the number of times that one number is contained in another is called *division*.

Example:

Divide   56648 by 8

Divisor

$$
\begin{array}{r}
7081 \text{ - quotient} \\
8\,\overline{\smash{)}56648} \text{ - dividend} \\
\underline{56} \\
64 \\
\underline{64} \\
8 \\
\underline{8} \\
\end{array}
$$

The number to be divided is called the *dividend*.
The number by which the dividend is divided is called the *divisor*.
The result of the division is the *quotient*.
When the divisor does not evenly divide the dividend, the number left over is called the *remainder*.

Checks or Proofs for Division

Method One:
   Multiply the quotient by the divisor and add the remainder.

Method Two:
   Similar to those for addition and multiplication:

Example:

$$
(1) \ldots 7 \quad 1\,540 \ldots 10^{(2)} \ldots 1^{(3)}
$$

$$
24{,}645 \div 16 \ = \ 16\,\overline{\smash{)}24{,}645} \qquad . \ 21^{(6)} \qquad 3^{(7)}
$$

$$
\begin{array}{r}
\underline{16} \\
86 \\
\underline{80} \\
64 \\
\underline{64} \\
5 \\
\end{array}
$$

$$
1 \times 7 = 7^{(4)}
$$
$$
\underline{+\ 5}
$$
$$
12 \ldots 3^{(5)}
$$

STEPS:

1. Add the numbers in the divisor:
   (Ex: 1 + 6 = 7)
2. Add the numbers in the quotient.
   (Ex: 1 + 5 + 4 + 0 = 10).
3. Add the numbers in step 2.
   (Ex: 1 + 0 = 1).
4. Multiply the sum of the numbers in the divisor by the sum of the numbers in the quotient or multiply step 1 × step 2.
   (Ex: 7 × 1 = 7)
5. Add the remainder 5 in the example to the number obtained in step 4.
   (Ex: 5 + 7 = 7)
6. Add the numbers in the dividend.
7. Continue to add until one number is obtained. The example is correct if the results in steps 5 and 7 are the same.

Exercise V

Divide and check the following:

1
6186 ÷ 6 = _____

2
8832 ÷ 8 = _____

3
3024 ÷ 12 = _____

4
246,454 ÷ 16 = _____

5
45,648 ÷ 48 = _____

6
5,434 ÷ 38 = _____

7
27,572 ÷ 61 = _____

8
9361 ÷ 37 = _____

9
28928 ÷ 84 = _____

10
38,781 ÷ 93 = _____

11
15688 ÷ 53 = _____

12
10,001 ÷ 34 = _____

13
252,576 ÷ 72 = _____

14
796,936 ÷ 428 = _____

15
562536 ÷ 468 = _____

16
897,468 ÷ 523 = _____

17
8,965,194 ÷ 678 = _____

18
50068514 ÷ 4001 = _____

19
837,336 ÷ 279 = _____

20
1,293,078 ÷ 2036 = _____

14

Problems

1. Miss Mead bought 9 jars of cleansing cream at $31.00 per doz., 7 boxes face powder at $19.00 per doz., 5 lipsticks at $14.00 per doz., 8 hair brushes at $16.40 per doz.
   a) Make a sales slip for the above order.
   b) Find the cost of the entire order.

   b) _____

2. Mr. Smith bought the following order: 6 doz. wave nets at $68.00 per gross, 3 qts. witch hazel at $13.00 per gal. and 3 lbs. shampoo granules costing $11.00 per 6 lbs., 18 permanent waves at $47.00 per doz.
   a) Make out a bill for this order.
   b) Find the cost of the order.

   b) _____

3. Miss Gold ordered the following supplies:
   3/4 doz. bottles of sanitizing tablets @ $25.00 per doz.
   1 qt. cuticle remover   @ 27.00 gal.
   1 qt. cuticle oil   @ 22.00 gal.
   1 lb. hand cream   @   3.88 per lb.

   a) Find the cost of the bill.
   b) How much does the hand cream cost per oz.? The remover per pint? The cuticle oil per pint?
   a) _____   b) _____   _____   _____

4. Assuming that 20 manicures can be given from the materials listed in 3b) above, find the cost per manicure of each material.

   _____

5. If there are 75 sanitizing tablets in each bottle
   a) How much does each tablet cost at $25.00 per doz. bottles?
   b) Find the cost of a gallon of sanitizing solution if 16 tablets are dissolved in a gallon of distilled water.

   a) _____   b) _____

6. a) Find the cost of 3 lbs of soap granules @ $24.65 per 10 lbs., 1/2 doz. spray lacquer @ $21.00 per dozen, 1 gal. polish remover @ $8.75 per gal., and 3/4 doz. tubes of scalp cream @ $23.50 per doz.

   Total cost _____

b) Find the cost of the polish remover per oz.

c) What is the cost per treatment if 1/2 tube of scalp cream is used per treatment?

b) _____   c) _____

7. Miss Mead pays Miss Adams $156.00 per week.
   She works 40 hours per week.
   a) How much does she receive per hour?
   b) Miss Adams was idle 4 hours and 30 minutes during the week. How much did Miss Mead pay for idle time?

   a) _____   b) _____

8. Miss Mead's expenses amounted to $2862.07 for the month of March.
   a) Figuring 21 working days for the month, how much did it cost per day to operate the business?
   b) How much per hour figuring 8 hours per day?

   a) _____   b) _____

9. a) How many shampoos can be given from 1 gallon of cream shampoo if it takes 2 oz. for each shampoo?
   b) If the shampoo costs $10.75 per gallon, how much does each treatment cost?
      Note: Refer to tables to compute the number of ounces in a gallon.

   a) _____   b) _____

10. Miss Mead's beauty salon is 34 ft. by 45 ft. How much will it cost her to cover her floor with linoleum if she pays $13.95 per sq. yd.?

    _____

FRACTIONS

A fraction is a quantity expressed in terms of numbers, one above and one below a horizontal line; for example $\frac{3}{2}$ or $\frac{4}{5}$. Sometimes, a slanting line is used; for example 2/3 or 4/5. These two numbers are called the *terms* of the fraction.

The upper number is called the *numerator,* and the lower number is called the *denominator.*

A *proper* fraction is one whose numerator is smaller than its denominator (2/3 or 4/5).

An *improper* fraction is one whose numerator is equal to or larger than its denominator (3/3, 3/2, 5/4).

A *mixed number* is the indicated sum of a whole number and a fraction (2 1/2, 4 3/8).

Reduction or Raising of Fractions

The value of a fraction is not changed by multiplying or dividing each term (the numerator and denominator) by the same number. A fraction may, therefore, be reduced to lower terms or raised to higher terms.

To raise fractions to higher terms, *multiply* both the numerator and the denominator by the same number.

Example: Raise 2/3 to higher terms.
               2/3 = 2/3 × 2/2 = 4/6

To reduce fractions to lower terms, *divide* both the numerator and the denominator by the same number.

Example: Reduce 32/40 to lower terms.
               32/40 ÷ 2/2 = 16/20 ÷ 2/2 = 8/10 ÷ 2/2 = 4/5

Exercise VI

Raise the following fractions to higher terms:
Example: 1/3 =   /9 = 1/3 × 3/3 = 3/9

1.
3/4 =   /16

2.
5/6 =   /30

3.
3/5 =   /30

4.
2/3 =   /48

5.
7/9 =   /45

6.
7/8 =   /24

7.
16/24 =   /48

8.
12/27 =   /81

9.
3/11 =   /121

10.
16/24 =   /96

11.
21/24 =   /120

12.
15/20 =   /100

13.
22/33 =   /198

14.
31/50 =   /200

15.
12/33 =   /99

16.
5/10 =   /1000

17.
3/14 =   /84

18.
13/28 =   /140

19.
3/8 =   /640

20.
4/5 =   /60

Exercise VII

Reduce the following fractions to lower terms:
Example: 3/9 = 3/9 ÷ 3/3 = 1/3

1.
15/18 = _____

2.
25/30 = _____

3.
14/18 = _____

4.
21/24 = _____

5.
36/48 = _____

6.
25/75 = _____

7.
39/42 = _____

8.
33/66 = _____

9.
81/96 = _____

10.
24/98 = _____

11.
90/100 = _____

12.
21/84 = _____

13.
18/81 = _____

14.
11/121 = _____

15.
36/64 = _____

16.
40/88 = _____

17.
39/91 = _____

18.
14/98 = _____

19.
54/117 = _____

20.
30/93 = _____

IMPROPER FRACTIONS

To reduce improper fractions to mixed numbers, divide the numerator by the denominator, the result will be a *mixed number*.

Example: 14/5 = 14 ÷ 5 = 2 4/5

Exercise VIII

Reduce the following to mixed numbers:

1.
11/3 = _____

2.
45/3 = _____

3.
26/4 = _____

4.
59/6 = _____

5.
57/8 = _____

6.
65/12 = _____

7.
121/11 = _____

8.
112/16 = _____

9.
60/11 = _____

10.
39/20 = _____

11.
105/18 = _____

12.
36/20 = _____

13.
87/36 = _____

14.
768/9 = _____

15.
95/12 = _____

16.
47/36 = _____

17.
156/12 = _____

18.
895/10 = _____

19.
37/7 = _____

20.
99/10 = _____

MIXED NUMBERS

To change a mixed number to an improper fraction, multiply the whole number by the denominator, add the numerator and write the number over the denominator.

Example: $8 \frac{4}{5} = \frac{8 \times 5 + 4}{5} = \frac{44}{5}$

Exercise IX

Change the following mixed numbers to improper fractions:

1.
$7 \frac{1}{6}$ = _____

2.
$8 \frac{4}{7}$ = _____

3.
$9 \frac{3}{5}$ = _____

4.
$5 \frac{2}{11}$ = _____

5.
$23 \frac{1}{3}$ = _____

6.
$9 \frac{3}{10}$ = _____

7.
$4 \frac{2}{11}$ = _____

8.
$22 \frac{2}{9}$ = _____

9.
$3 \frac{9}{20}$ = _____

10.
$5 \frac{3}{8}$ = _____

11.
$9 \frac{3}{8}$ = _____

12.
$8 \frac{5}{12}$ = _____

13.
$17 \frac{3}{10}$ = _____

14.
$12 \frac{1}{4}$ = _____

15.
$18 \frac{3}{8}$ = _____

16.
$25 \frac{7}{8}$ = _____

17.
$72 \frac{2}{3}$ = _____

18.
$181 \frac{2}{7}$ = _____

19.
$256 \frac{2}{3}$ = _____

20.
$346 \frac{2}{9}$ = _____

COMMON DENOMINATORS

When two or more fractions have the same denominator, they are said to have a common denominator. Example: 1/8, 3/8, 5/8

The *least common denominator* of two or more fractions is the smallest number that contains each denominator without a remainder. Example: 2/3, 3/4, 7/8

The least common *denominator,* or the lowest possible figure that can be divided by 3, 4, 8, evenly, is 24. —— $\frac{2}{3} = \frac{16}{24}$; $\frac{3}{4} = \frac{18}{24}$; $\frac{7}{8} = \frac{21}{24}$

To find the least common denominator use the highest denominator and see if it contains the others. If not, double it, then try again. If not, triple it and so on until it does. In the example above 8 is not evenly divisible by 3; 8 doubled or 16 is not; 8 tripled or 24 is. Therefore, the L.C.D. is 24.

Exercise X

Find the least common denominator (LCD) of the following:

1.
3/4; 4/5 = _____

2.
1/7; 2/3; 1/21 = _____

3.
2/3; 3/5; 7/15 = _____

4.
1/4; 3/20; 7/10 = _____

5.
2/3; 5/8; 1/6 = _____

6.
4/15; 5/6; 3/10 = _____

7.
3/4; 7/12; 5/144 = _____

8.
5/8; 2/3; 5/6 = _____

9.
2/9; 9/16; 3/4; 2/3 = _____

10.
2/5; 1/2; 5/24 = _____

11.
5/6; 2/3; 7/51 = _____

12.
4/9; 2/3; 9/56; 5/12 = _____

13.
1/3; 9/16; 11/20 = _____

14.
5/9; 4/15; 2/7 = _____

15.
11/12; 3/16; 1/3; 3/8 = _____

16.
3/4; 5/8; 6/7; 1/10 = _____

ADDITION OF FRACTIONS

To add fractions, they must first be changed to similar fractions having the least common denominator.

Example: $1/2 + 2/3 = 3/6 + 4/6 = 7/6$ or $1\,1/6$

Exercise XI

1.

$2/3 + 1/2 + 5/6 = $ _____

2.

$1/2 + 2/3 + 1/4 + 5/8 = $ _____

3.

$3/4 + 4/5 + 3/10 = $ _____

4.

$2/3 + 3/8 + 5/6 + 1/4 = $ _____

5.

$3/6 + 5/8 + 3/4 + 1/2 = $ _____

6.

$3/20 + 3/5 + 7/10 = $ _____

7.

$4/9 + 8/27 + 2/3 = $ _____

8.

$9/16 + 5/12 + 1/4 = $ _____

9.

$7/15 + 1/3 + 3/4 + 2/5 = $ _____

10.

$7/8 + 4/5 + 3/10 + 1/2 = $ _____

11.

$8/9 + 1/3 + 5/6 + 1/2 = $ _____

12.

$2/3 + 4/15 + 2/5 + 9/30 = $ _____

13.

$5/7 + 2/9 + 2/3 + 5/9 = $ _____

14.

$5/6 + 4/9 + 5/21 = $ _____

15.

$3/5 + 4/9 + 7/15 = $ _____

16.

$7/12 + 9/10 + 1/6 = $ _____

17.

$11/18 + 7/15 + 3/15 = $ _____

18.

$8/45 + 2/9 + 4/5 = $ _____

19.

$5/120 + 7/12 + 3/8 = $ _____

20.

$7/90 + 3/5 + 2/9 + 8/45 = $ _____

Addition of Mixed Numbers

Change the following mixed numbers to fractions and add. Reduce the answer to a mixed number.

Example: $3\ 1/12\ +\ 1\ 4/15\ =\ \dfrac{185\ +\ 76}{60}\ =$ _____

$\dfrac{261}{60}\ =\ 4\ 7/20$

Exercise XII

1.
6 1/2 + 8 1/3 = _____

2.
10 5/6 + 3 1/2 = _____

3.
6 2/3 + 8 1/2 = _____

4.
14 3/4 + 6 1/2 + 2 2/3 = _____

5.
56 7/8 + 5 3/5 + 2 1/10 = _____

6.
2 1/5 + 7 5/6 + 1 3/10 = _____

7.
3 1/2 + 7/8 + 5 2/16 + 8 3/4 = ____

8.
2 3/4 + 5 5/6 + 7 3/8 + 5 2/3 =____

9.
35 1/2 + 11 5/6 + 7 2/3 + 9 1/4 =__

10.
7 1/5 + 8 4/15 + 7 5/6 = _____

11.
37 + 8 2/3 + 5 + 5/9 = _____

12.
6 1/24 + 4 1/3 + 5 = _____

13.
7 2/3 + 9 5/12 + 7 + 3/4 = _____

14.
5 3/8 + 15 1/2 + 9 5/6 = _____

15.
75 + 6 2/3 + 8 7/15 =_____

16.
5 1/2 + 16 + 4 5/7 + 9 = _____

17.
19 5/8 + 4 5/6 + 5 1/2 + 3 = _____

18.
18 + 3 15/16 + 7 1/4 + 5 1/8 =____

19.
27 + 7/15 + 8 2/3 + 4 1/5 = _____

20.
25 + 1/6 + 7 1/5 + 8 5/12 + 9 + 10 4/15 = _____

23

SUBTRACTIONS OF FRACTIONS

To subtract fractions, they must be reduced to simple fractions having a common denominator. Write the difference over the common denominator, and reduce the result to the lowest terms.

Example: $7/8 - 1/4 = 7/8 - 2/8 = 5/8$

Exercise XIII

1.
$3/8 - 5/16 =$ _____

2.
$5/12 - 1/4 =$ _____

3.
$4/9 - 8/27 =$ _____

4.
$17/20 - 3/4 =$ _____

5.
$5/9 - 3/7 =$ _____

6.
$31/45 - 2/3 =$ _____

7.
$5/6 - 3/4 =$ _____

8.
$2/3 - 7/33 =$ _____

9.
$5\ 3/4 - 2\ 1/6 =$ _____

10.
$4\ 3/10 - 3/4 =$ _____

11.
$6\ 2/3 - 3\ 1/4 =$ _____

12.
$5\ 1/24 - 4\ 1/3 =$ _____

13.
$8\ 2/3 - 5\ 1/2 =$ _____

14.
$85\ 3/9 - 72\ 1/2 =$ _____

15.
$152\ 7/8 - 5\ 3/5 =$ _____

16.
$189\ 2/15 - 15\ 3/5 =$ _____

17.
$12 - 3\ 1/3 =$ _____

18.
$22\ 2/3 - 10\ 11/12 =$ _____

19.
$85 - 75\ 1/2 =$ _____

20.
$385 - 214\ 1/5 =$ _____

MULTIPLICATION OF FRACTIONS

To multiply fractions, change all mixed numbers to improper fractions. Whole numbers must be treated as having 1 for the denominator. Cancel out numerators into denominators or vice versa wherever possible. Multiply the numerators that are left. Multiply the denominators that are left. Reduce the fractions to a mixed number or smallest fraction.

Example:

$$\frac{1}{3}\times\frac{2}{3}\times\frac{3}{4} = \frac{1\times2\times3}{3\times3\times4} = \frac{1\times\cancel{2}\times\cancel{3}}{3\times\cancel{3}\times\cancel{4}} = \frac{1}{6}$$

$$\frac{3}{5}\times2\frac{1}{2}\times1\frac{7}{24} = \frac{3\times5\times31}{5\times2\times24} = \frac{\cancel{3}\times\cancel{5}\times31}{\cancel{5}\times2\times\cancel{24}} = \frac{31}{16} = 1\frac{15}{16}$$

Exercise XIV

1.
3/5 × 3/4 = _____

2.
7/12 × 4/7 = _____

3.
8/15 × 7/8 × 3/4 = _____

4.
5/14 × 7/12 × 3/5 = _____

5.
2 1/4 × 1 3/5 = _____

6.
14 1/3 × 16 = _____

7.
2/9 × 3/16 × 5/8 = _____

8.
14 1/3 × 16 = _____

9.
5/16 × 2 2/3 × 4/15 = _____

10.
5/9 × 9/10 × 11/12 × 6/7 = _____

11.
7/8 × 11/16 × 8/11 × 4 4/7 = _____

12.
6 1/2 × 4 1/3 × 3 = _____

13.
44 2/3 × 10 1/5 = _____

14.
6 3/4 × 4 1/3 × 4/5 = _____

15.
22 2/5 × 12 1/4 = _____

16.
65 3/4 × 15 1/8 = _____

17.
21 2/3 × 11 3/5 =·_____

18.
24 3/8 × 5/12 × 2/5 = _____

DIVISION OF FRACTIONS

To divide one fraction by another, invert the divisor, reduce the fraction where possible, and multiply.

Examples:

$$(1) \quad \frac{3}{5} \div \frac{7}{15} = \frac{3}{\underset{1}{\cancel{5}}} \times \frac{\overset{3}{\cancel{15}}}{7} = \frac{3}{1} \times \frac{3}{7} = \frac{9}{7} = 1\frac{2}{7}$$

$$(2) \quad 2\frac{1}{4} \div \frac{1}{2} = \frac{9}{4} \times \frac{2}{1} = \frac{9}{\underset{2}{\cancel{4}}} \times \frac{\overset{1}{\cancel{2}}}{1} = \frac{9}{2} = 4\frac{1}{2}$$

Exercise XV

Divide the following:

1.
5/7 ÷ 3/7 = _____

2.
4/9 ÷ 2/3 = _____

3.
5/7 ÷ 1/14 = _____

4.
9 3/4 ÷ 3/8 = _____

5.
2 8/9 ÷ 7 1/3 = _____

6.
235 ÷ 3 3/4 = _____

7.
8 ÷ 16/25 = _____

8.
6 3/8 ÷ 1/4 = _____

9.
99 5/16 ÷ 6 1/4 = _____

10.
85 ÷ 9 3/4 = _____

11.
97 3/7 ÷ 13 1/2 = _____

12.
76 1/4 ÷ 8 1/8 = _____

13.
125 ÷ 4/5 = _____

14.
228 ÷ 1/4 = _____

15.
84 1/3 ÷ 9 1/3 = _____

16.
56 1/2 ÷ 7 3/4 = _____

17.
328 2/3 ÷ 31 1/3 = _____

18.
446 3/8 ÷ 28 1/2 = _____

Problems

1. How many booth curtains can be made from 28 yards of material if it takes 3 1/2 yards for one curtain? _____

2. How much will each of the above curtains cost at $3.50 per yard? _____

3. If 4 2/3 yards of booth curtain material cost $22.00, how much will 5 1/3 yards cost? _____

4. One dozen wave clips cost $2.50 per dozen. How much will 3 1/2 dozen cost? _____

5. If 1/4 yard of gauze used in giving a facial costs $.20, how much will 6 1/2 yards cost? _____

6. Mr. Martin bought the following supplies for his beauty salon:

   3/4 dozen bottles setting lotion at $21.00 per doz.;
   1 1/2 doz. jars cream at $30.00 per dozen;
   1/3 doz. hand lotion at $19.00 per dozen.

   Make out a bill and find the cost of the above order.

   _____

7. A cosmetologist was paid a regular weekly salary of $156.00. Her tips for one week amounted to 2/5 of her salary. How much money did she receive for the week?

   _____

8. A cosmetologist must double her salary before her employer can realize a profit on her services. Miss Adams is paid a salary of $156.00 per week. The first week she performed services which amounted to 3/5 that amount.

   a) How much service income did she produce? _____
   b) How much did her employer lose on her week's work? _____

9. Mr. Jenkins bought the following items to replenish his stock of merchandise for resale:

1/2 doz. creams	@ $34.00 per dozen
2/3 doz. powders	@ 31.00 per dozen
1/4 doz. skin lotions	@ 36.20 per dozen
7/12 doz. eye shadow	@ 21.00 per dozen
1/4 doz. lipstick	@ 31.00 per dozen
1 only lip brush	@ 21.00 per dozen

   a. How many dozen items did he buy? _____
   b. What is the cost of the entire order? _____

10. A large tub of shampoo jelly weighs 53 3/4 lbs. The empty tub weighs 5 1/2 lbs. What is the cost of the shampoo at $.78 per lb.? _____

11. A beauty supply salesman bought gas and oil on a trip as follows: 12 gallons @ $1.60 1/2 per gallon, 15 gallons @ $1.61 1/2 per gallon, 14 gallons at $1.63 1/2 per gallon and 2 quarts of oil at $1.90 per quart.

   The gas tank on his car registered 13 gallons when he started for which he paid $1.60 1/2 per gallon. When he reached home he had 8 gallons of gas left.

   a) Find the total quantity of gas used on the trip. _____

   b) Find the cost of gas and oil for the trip. _____

12. The salesman in problem #11 checked the speedometer on his car at the beginning of the trip and found it read 27,243 miles. At the end of the trip it read 27,963.

   a. How many miles did he travel? _____
   b. Find the average cost of gas per mile on the trip. _____

13. Miss Mead employed a carpenter to build 4 shelves of equal length in her storage room. He bought a board 14 2/3 ft. long. How long was each shelf? _____

DECIMALS

A decimal is a fraction whose denominator is 10, 100, 1000, or any other power of 10. A *decimal point* is used to indicate the denominator as follows:

4/10 is written .4;   4/100 = .04;   7/1000 = .007.

Common fractions may be changed to decimal fractions and vice versa.

To change a common fraction to a *decimal*, write the numerator, place a decimal point after it, add zeros, and divide by the denominator.

Example: Change 3/8 to a decimal:

$$\begin{array}{r} .375 \\ 8\overline{)3.000} \\ 24 \\ \overline{60} \\ 56 \\ \overline{40} \\ 40 \end{array}$$

Thus 3/8 = .375

1/10 or .1 is read one tenth
1/100 or .01 is read one one hundredth
1/1000 or .001 is read as one one thousandth

When reading decimals, read the number as a whole and then name the denominator which has as many zeros as there are places to the right of the decimal point.

Example: .4536 written as a fraction is:
        4536/10000 and is read:
        four thousand five hundred thirty-six ten thousandths

Exercise XVI

Write out the following decimals as in the above example:

1.
.7 _____

2.
.01 _____

3.
.343 _____

4.
.0238 _____

5.
7.46 _____

6.
8.263 _____

7.
503.47 _____

8.
4.683 _____

9.
5.2004 _____

10.
7.5576 _____

Exercise XVII

Change the following common fractions to decimals:
(Carry to 3 decimal places and indicate by a plus (+) sign if there is a remainder.)

1.

$1/2 =$ _____

2.

$3/4 =$ _____

3.

$3/8 =$ _____

4.

$5/8 =$ _____

5.

$11/16 =$ _____

6.

$9/10 =$ _____

7.

$12/15 =$ _____

8.

$27/36 =$ _____

9.

$33/44$ _____

10.

$49/63$ _____

11.

$25/45$ _____

12.

$64/72$ _____

13.

$32/40$ _____

14.

$45/54$ _____

15.

$18/19$ _____

16.

$21/32$ _____

17.

$2/9$ _____

18.

$5/6$ _____

19.

$1/6$ _____

20.

$1/15$ _____

Exercise XVIII

To change a decimal to a common fraction, write it as a common fraction and reduce it to lowest terms:

Example: $.75 = 75/100 = 3/4$

$$.26 \, 2/3 = \frac{26 \, 2/3}{100} = \frac{26 \, 2/3 \times 3}{100 \times 3} = \frac{80}{300} = \frac{4}{15}$$

1.	**2.**	**3.**	**4.**
.5 _____	.05 _____	.005 _____	.95 _____
5.	**6.**	**7.**	**8.**
.16 _____	.40 _____	.55 _____	.125 _____
9.	**10.**	**11.**	**12.**
.026 _____	.225 _____	.625 _____	.008 _____
13.	**14.**	**15.**	**16.**
.9375 _____	.875 _____	.5304 _____	.2 2/3 _____
17.	**18.**	**19.**	**20.**
.83 1/3 _____	.16 2/3 _____	.12 1/2 _____	.67 1/2 _____

Addition and Subtraction of Decimals

To add or subtract decimals, write decimal points directly under each other.

Example:
```
$ 4.50        $10.50
 19.00       - 8.75
  2.70       _____
_____        $ 1.75
$26.20
```

Exercise XIX

Add the following decimals:

1.

.25 + 5.30 = _____

2.

4.32 + .65 + 34.70 = _____

3.

.09 + 8.76 + 5.50 = _____

4.

6 + 3.39 + 8 = _____

5.

.45 + 16 + 6.7 = _____

6.

11.65 + 14 1/3 = _____

7.

4.5 + .025 + 16.03 = _____

8.

16.50 + 4.06 + .325 = _____

9.

.972 + .65 + 34.70 = _____

10.

8.40 + 223.02 + .506 = _____

Exercise XX

Subtract the following:

1.

18.76 − 9.49 = _____

2.

7.086 − .543 = _____

3.

1.76 − .94 = _____

4.

369.40 − 198.59 = _____

5.

90.078 − 8.008 = _____

6.

4.2306 − 1.74 = _____

7.

67.5508 − 44.402 = _____

8.

261.45 − 7.0625 = _____

9.

468.32 − 423.59 = _____

10.

321.42 − 162.43 = _____

MULTIPLICATION OF DECIMALS

To multiply decimals, multiply as if by whole numbers. Then point off in the product (counting from right to left) as many decimal places as there are in the multiplicand and the multiplier.

Example: 3.24 × 1.6 =

$$
\begin{array}{r}
3.24 \quad \text{(2 places)} \\
\times 1.6 \quad \text{(1 place)} \\
\hline
1944 \\
324 \quad\;\; \\
\hline
5.184 \quad \text{(3 places)}
\end{array}
$$

If the product does not contain as many decimal places as are in both the multiplier and the multiplicand, zeros must be written to the left of the product to make up the required number of places.

Example:

$$
\begin{array}{r}
.032 \\
\times \;\; .04 \\
\hline
.00128 \quad \text{(5 places)}
\end{array}
$$

Exercise XXI

Multiply the following:

1.
3.28 × 4.1 = _____

2.
3.04 × 2.3 = _____

3.
62.9 × 3.7 = _____

4.
839.5 × .54 = _____

5.
35.42 × 7.6 = _____

6.
.275 × 9.4 = _____

7.
73.26 × .014 = _____

8.
6.32 × .065 = _____

9.
3.045 × .083 = _____

10.
.4375 × 1.34 = _____

DIVISION OF DECIMALS

To divide a decimal by a whole number, first place the decimal point in the quotient directly above that in the dividend and place figures in the quotient directly above the *last figure* of partial dividend. If necessary, use zeros after the decimal point in the quotient.

Example: $1.0520 \div 3 = 3/\overline{1.0520}$ with quotient $.3506 +$

To divide a decimal by a decimal multiply both the dividend and the divisor by such a power of 10 as shall make the divisor a whole number.

Divide and write the decimal point in the quotient as soon as the decimal point in the dividend is reached.

Example: $.74 \div .3 = .3./\overline{.7.4000}$ with quotient $2.4666 +$

Example: $7 \div .25 = .25./\overline{700.}$ with quotient $28.$
$$\underline{50}$$
$$200$$
$$\underline{200}$$

Exercise XXII

Divide the following to the *third* decimal place and check:

1.
$63.9 \div 3.7 = $ _____

2.
$5.64 \div 8 = $ _____

3.
$600 \div .06 = $ _____

4.
$36.42 \div 7.8 = $ _____

5.
$4.67 \div .325 = $ _____

6.
$57.6 \div .048 = $ _____

7.
$15.52 \div 96 = $ _____

8.
$78.4 \div .65 = $ _____

9.
$62.23 \div .23 = $ _____

10.
$19.26 \div .031 = $ _____

Problems

1. A jobber of beauty supplies sold a quantity of shampoo granules and received $232.00 for selling them.
   - a) If his commission was $.41 per lb., how many lbs. did he sell? _____
   - b) The price per lb. was $2.20. What is the total value of the granules? _____

2. Miss Jenkins worked in a beauty salon from 8:00 a.m. to 5:00 p.m. with one hour off for lunch.
   At $3.95 per hour, how much did she earn in 5 days? _____

3.
   - a) If combs cost $.95½ each, how many dozen combs can be bought for $28.90? _____
   - b) The selling price is $2.85 per comb. All but two combs were sold. How much profit was made on the combs sold? _____

4. Miss Mead wanted her beauty salon redecorated. She consulted a painter who gave her an estimate of $475.00 with materials furnished.
   Miss Mead decided to buy the materials herself and hire the painter at $10.75 per hour. The varnish cost $53.50, paint $66.34 and other materials $22.60. The painter worked 6 hours on Monday, 5 hours on Tuesday and 7 hours on Wednesday.
   - a) Find the total cost. _____
   - b) How much more or less than $475.00 was this? _____

5.
   - a) If two cosmetologists waste ½ oz. of shampoo on each patron shampooed, how much do they waste doing 8 patrons in a day? _____
   - b) Counting 250 working days per year, and an average of 8 shampoos per day, how many gallons of shampoo do these cosmetologists waste in a year? _____
   - c) The shampoo costs $9.75 per gallon. How much money does the employer lose per year on the cosmetologists' wastefulness? _____

6. Mr. Johnson bought 750 calendars to give to his patrons as a means of advertising. The price of the calendars was $185.75 per 1000.
   - a) How much did each calendar cost? _____
   - b) What was the total cost of the order? _____

7. Miss Scott's regular work week is 40 hours, and she receives a salary of $152.00. She receives $5.70 per hour for each hour overtime she works. On Tuesday she worked 2½ hours overtime, Thursday 3 hours and on Friday 1½ hours overtime.

a) How much overtime pay did she receive? _____

b) She received $35.75 in tips besides her salary. How much did she receive in all for the week? _____

PERCENT

The term "percent" means "by the hundred" or so many "hundredths" of anything.

Use decimals whose denominators are 100.

Example: 28/100 = .28 = 28 percent or 28%.

Percents are of use for comparison. A merchant finds that this year he made a profit of 25% as compared with 20% last year. He may note that costs have gone up or down a certain percent; or that a certain percent of goods sold are returned, etc.

Numbers expressed as percent can be expressed as fractions or decimals.

To change a decimal to a percent, write the decimal as hundredths, omit the word *hundredths* and write *percent* to the right of the number.

Examples:

$$.40 = 40 \text{ hundredths} = 40 \text{ percent} = 40\%$$

$$.1 = 10 \text{ hundredths} = 10 \text{ percent} = 10\%$$

$$.125 = 12.5 \ (12\tfrac{1}{2}) \text{ hundredths} = 12\tfrac{1}{2} \text{ percent} = 12\tfrac{1}{2}\%$$

$$.1625 = 16.25 \ (16\tfrac{1}{4}) \text{ hundredths} = 16\tfrac{1}{4} \text{ percent} = 16\tfrac{1}{4}\%$$

$$2.23 = 223 \text{ hundredths} = 223 \text{ percent} = 223\%$$

Exercise XXIII

Change the following to percents:

1.
.25 = _____

2.
.18 = _____

3.
.05 = _____

4.
13 1/2 = _____

5.
1.35 = _____

6.
.155 = _____

7.
1.625 = _____

8.
2.25 = _____

9.
1.005 = _____

10.
3.0525 = _____

Change Common Fractions to Percent

To change a common fraction to a percent, write the fraction as hundredths in decimal form and then as percent.

Examples:

$$1/3 = \frac{100}{300} = .33\ 1/3 = 33\ 1/3\%$$

$$5/9 = \frac{500}{900} = .55\ 5/9 = 55\ 5/9\%$$

$$1\ 1/4 = \frac{125}{100} = 1.25 = 125\%$$

Exercise XXIV

Write the following as percents:

1.

2/3 = _____

2.

7/8 = _____

3.

3/16 = _____

4.

1/8 = _____

5.

5/7 = _____

6.

4/7 = _____

7.

6/25 = _____

8.

2 2/3 = _____

9.

1 1/8 = _____

10.

3 2/5 = _____

Change Percent to Decimal

To change a percent to a decimal write the percent as hundredths and then write it using the decimal point to show hundredths.

Example: $$55\% = \frac{55}{100} = .55$$

$$6\% = \frac{6}{100} = .06$$

$$120\% = \frac{120}{100} = 1.20$$

Exercise XXV

Change the following to decimal fractions:

1.
.8% = _____

2.
5% = _____

3.
20% = _____

4.
75% = _____

5.
2 1/2% = ____

6.
16 2/3% = ____

7.
3/8% = _____

8.
150% = _____

9.
.01% = _____

10.
350% = _____

Change Percent to Common Fraction

To change a percent to a common fraction, the percent must be changed to a decimal; then change the decimal to a common fraction and reduce it to its lowest terms.

Examples: $25\% = .25 = \dfrac{25}{100} = 1/4$

$1/2\% = .0050 = \dfrac{50}{10000} = 1/200$

$3\ 1/2\% = .035 = \dfrac{35}{1000} = 7/200$

$7\% = .07 = \dfrac{7}{100}$

Exercise XXVI

Change the following to common fractions and reduce to lowest terms:

1.
.35% = _____

2.
1/3% = _____

3.
18% = _____

4.
.6% = _____

5.
240% = _____

6.
175% = _____

7.
2/3% = _____

8.
2 1/2% = _____

9.
2.8% = _____

10.
15.6 1/4% = _____

PERCENTAGE

Percentage means so many hundredths of anything.

Example: 10% of $1.00 = $\dfrac{10}{100}$ of 100 = $ .10

In percentage the following terms are commonly used:

Base (B), *Rate* (R), and *Percentage* (P).

The number upon which the percent is to be figured is called the *base*; thus, in taking 5% of $100.00, $100.00 is the base.

The percent or the part taken is called the *rate*. In taking 5% of $100.00, the rate is 5%.

The result obtained by multiplying the base by the rate is known as the *percentage*; thus, in taking 5% of $100.00, the percentage is $5.00.

Percentage is found by multiplying the *Base* (B) by the *Rate* (R).

P = B × R

Example: $180.00 (B) × 50% (R) = (P)
$\qquad\qquad$ 180.00 × .50 = $90.00 (P)

Exercise XXVII

1.

25% of 160.00 = _____

2.

6% of $480.00 = _____

3.

1/2% of $500.00 = _____

4.

12% of $600.00 = _____

5.

55% of $555.00 = _____

6.

5 1/2% of $42.50 = _____

7.

32% of $2900.00 = _____

8.

16 1/4% of $3200.00 = _____

9.

125% of $15.00 = _____

10.

3 3/4% of $3725.00 = _____

Problems

1. Miss Mead bought new equipment for her beauty salon. She paid $965.50 for it. The first year it depreciated 10%.
   a. How much was the first year's depreciation?
   b. How much was the equipment worth at the end of the first year?

a._____   b._____

2. Mr. Jenkins bought for his beauty salon the following: 1 1/2 doz. cleansing cream at $19.50 per dozen, 3/4 dozen face powder at $21.00 per dozen, 3/4 dozen cold waves at $36.20 per dozen. He paid cash for the order thereby receiving a 2% discount.

   How much did he gain by paying cash? _____

3. A beauty salon did $65,500 worth of business last year. This year the business increased 12 1/2%.

   How much was realized from this year's business? _____

4. The owner of a beauty salon hired two new cosmetologists at $156.00 per week each. The first week the owner lost 50% of the salary on one and 65% on the other because of lack of services rendered. How much money was lost on the two employees the first week?

   _____

5. The owner of a beauty salon averaged a 25% loss on two new cosmetologists' salaries for a period of 6 weeks. Each cosmetologist was paid $160.00. What was the loss for the six weeks?

   _____

6. A hairdryer costing $247.50 depreciated 10% each year for 5 years. What is its value at the end of that time?

   _____

7. The income of a beauty salon was $45,654 for one year. 45% of that amount was paid out in salaries.
   How much was paid in salaries? _____

8. The beauty salon in the problem above had an income of $45,654 for one year. The expenses were:
   Salaries 45%; Rent 15%; Supplies, laundry, advertising and other expenses 20%.
   a. What were the expenses for the year?
   b. How much does the owner have left for himself?

a._____   b._____

9. Miss Denton's laundry bill for a year was $665.00, supplies $2982.00 and salaries $16,856.00.

   The employees wasted 2% of the laundry by using towels unnecessarily and 10% of the supplies by carelessness. 8% of the salaries paid was for idle unproductive time.
   How much did Miss Denton lose on those three items?

41

Finding the Rate

Given the *Base* and the *Percent* —— find the *Rate*.

$R = P \div B$ or $R = \dfrac{P}{B}$

Example: What percent is $12.00 of $60.00?

$R = \$12.00 \ (P) \div \$60.00 \ (B)$

$R = \dfrac{12}{60} = \dfrac{1}{5}$

$R = \dfrac{1}{5} = 20\%$

Exercise XXVIII

What percent is:

1.

$150 of $1200 _____

2.

$22.50 of $150.00 _____

3.

$465 of $750 _____

4.

$600 of $1875 _____

5.

4185 of 4500 _____

6.

1500 of 4500 _____

7.

$5.50 of $2200 _____

8.

$50 of $7500 _____

9.

$437.50 of $1750 _____

10.

200 of 3200 _____

Problems

1. Miss Mead bought an order of cosmetics amounting to $247.60 for resale in her beauty salon. She sold most of them and made a profit of $79.20.

   What percent profit did she make? _____

2. A beauty salon did $48,560 worth of business in one year. The payroll amounted to $20,860.00.

   What percent of the income was the payroll? _____

3. A beauty salon owner made an investment of $7200 and received an income of $306 from it.

   What was the percent profit? _____

4. Mr. James carries a mortgage on his property amounting to $9880. He paid $543.40 interest on the mortgage.

   What is the rate of interest paid? _____

5. A beauty salon owner bought equipment amounting to $1450. He paid $652.50 as a down payment.

   What percent of the bill did he pay? _____

6. Miss Scott spent $3,585 to advertise her business in one year. The receipts for the year were $25,905.

   What was the percent spent for advertising? _____

7. A supply salesman sold equipment to a beauty salon owner amounting to $3557.45. He received $547.30 for his share of the sale.

   What percent of the amount did he receive? _____

8. Mrs. Jones started in business without previous experience in figuring costs. At the end of the first year she was surprised to find that her income was $14,589.60 and her expenses were as follows:

   Supplies $3355.60   Salaries $6127.63   Rent $1750.75   Laundry, etc. $2042.54

   a. What percent of the income was spent for supplies?   a. _____
   b. For salaries?   b. _____
   c. For rent?   c. _____
   d. For laundry and other expenses?   d. _____
   e. Approximately what percent profit did she realize   e. _____
      on all her efforts for the year?

9. By careful study and management Mrs. Jones increased her business income to $28,342.57 the second year and her expenses to $12,520.45.

   What was her percent profit for the second year? _____

Finding the Base

Given the *Percentage and Rate* find the *Base*.

$$B = P \div R \text{ or } B = \frac{P}{R}$$

Example: 12 (P) is 25% (R) of what?

$$B = 12 \div .25 \text{ or } 12 \div \frac{1}{4} \text{ or } 12 \times \frac{4}{1} = 48 \text{ (B)}$$

Exercise XXIX

What is the amount or *Base* in the following?

1.

$75 is 12% = _____

2.

$15.00 is 15% = _____

3.

$5.25 is 50% = _____

4.

$24.00 is 33 1/3% = _____

5.

$60.00 is 37 1/2% = _____

6.

$840 is 5.2% = _____

7.

720 is 15% = _____

8.

$1200 is 24% = _____

9.

480 is 6 1/4% = _____

10.

$640 is 18 3/4% = _____

Problems

1. Mrs. Herd allows her employees 25% discount on the cosmetics they buy in her salon. By this reduction one employee saved $7.30.

   How much did she pay for the cosmetics? _____

2. Miss Adams' employer deducted 6% from her salary for insurance. It amounted to $9.36 for one week.

   What is Miss Adams' salary for the week? _____

3. Mrs. Jones got a loan from the bank to pay on the remodeling of her beauty salon and paid 17% interest on it. The interest amounted to $684.00 for the first year.

   What is the amount of the loan? _____

4. Miss Mead was allowed 2% off her bill for supplies for paying cash if paid within ten days. She saved $12.75 on the order.

   What was the amount of the order? _____

5. A beauty supply salesman received $1150 in one month on his sales. His commission is 30% on all sales.

   Find the amount of his sales for the month. _____

6. A piece of equipment for a beauty salon had depreciated 85% at the end of 10 years. The depreciation amounted to $375.00.

   What was the original price of the equipment? _____

7. A beauty salon owner ordered supplies. He paid $500 which was 35% of the order.

   What was the amount of the order? _____

8. Mrs. Jenkins' expenses for one year were $5460 which amounted to 45% of her income.

   How much was her income for the year? _____

9. Miss Harding opened a new beauty salon. She paid $2450 cash on her equipment. This was 30% of the entire amount.

   How much did she pay for the equipment? _____

COMMERCIAL DISCOUNTS

A *discount* is the amount deducted from a certain price. It is usually stated in terms of percent.

For example: 2% deducted from the price for cash payment.

Three types of commercial discounts, according to the purpose to be served, are *trade discounts, cash discounts,* and *quantity discounts.*

Trade discount is a discount or percentage deducted from the list price of particular trade merchandise. It is given to those in that trade for use or for resale.

Example: 33 1/3% off list price of cosmetics for resale.

Quantity Discount is a discount allowed on a given list price for purchasing a certain number or quantity.

Example: Pads of sales slips $5.00 for 100, 25% discount on 1000.

Cash Discount is a discount allowed a purchaser for paying the sum of a bill within a certain time.

Example: Total amount of bill $35.00, 2% discount for cash.

List price is the price of an article at which it is sold to the public.

Net price is the price of an article after the discount has been made.

Problems

1. Miss Mead bought the following supplies for use in her beauty salon:

   1 gallon shampoo, $12.75; 10 lbs. hair pins, $14.50; 1 dozen cold wave lotion $37.20 and 3 lbs. facial cleansing cream, $11.50.

   She was given a 2% discount for payment within 10 days.

   What was the amount of the check Miss Mead sent in payment for the supplies received?

   _____

2. A window display figure costs $124.50 each; a 25% discount is given on two figures purchased at the same time.

   A 30% discount is given on three figures purchased at the same time.

   a. How much does each cost by purchasing two at the same time? _____

   b. How much is saved on each? _____

   c. How much is saved by buying three at the same time? _____

3. Mrs. Jones bought an order of supplies amounting to $36.45. The terms of payment are 3/10, N/60.

   How much did she save by taking advantage of the discount? _____

   Note:
   3/10 means 3% discount if paid within 10 days. N/60 means the bill must be paid on or before the end of 60 days with no discount allowed. Considerable money may be saved in a year's time by taking advantage of all discounts.

4. Miss Jackson ordered supplies for her beauty salon as follows: 3 gallons shampoo at $12.75 per gallon; 9 dozen combs at $2.95 dozen; 4 lbs. cotton at $2.75 per lb., 12 dozen boxes hair pins at $2.95 per dozen boxes; 3 dozen nets at $4.50 per dozen.

   She was given an 8% discount on the order.

   a. What was the amount of her discount? _____

   b. How much did she pay? _____

5. A beauty supply dealer bought equipment from the manufacturer amounting to $1216.50 which he would sell to the beauty salons. The manufacturer gave trade discounts of 30% and 10%.

   Find the net price of the equipment. _____

6. Miss Mead bought 4 manicure tables with chairs for $135.00 each. The terms were 12% discount if paid at the end of 30 days. She paid cash in 10 days in which case the discount was 1 1/2 times the rate of discount.

   How much did she pay for the tables? _____

7. Miss Mead bought 1 gross bottles of P.W. solution at $37.20 per dozen. She was given a 15% discount on the order. When the order was received, 8 bottles were broken for which she did not pay.

   How much did she pay? _____

8. Miss Mead wanted to buy a new cash register for her beauty salon. One company offered a new one for $1150.00 and $95.00 as trade-in value on her old one, less discounts of 20% and 10%.

   Another company offered a new cash register for $1235.00 with trade-in value of $75.00 on her old one less 25% and 15% discount.

   a. Which is the better offer? _____

   b. How much better? _____

9. Miss Mead's beauty salon was 30 ft. wide and 45 ft. long. She had the floor covered with linoleum at $10.75 per square yard. She was given a 12% discount for cash. How much did she pay to have the floor covered? _____

PROFIT AND LOSS

Any legitimate business is a service to the community. Every business must make a substantial profit in order to exist. Without profit it could not pay the expenses and leave enough money for the owner's livelihood plus an interest on his investment.

Profit

Profit or *Gain* is the amount received over and above cost or expenses. It is figured at a given rate and added to the cost, thus making the selling price more than the cost.

Gross Profit = Net Sales − Cost of Goods Sold

Example: An order of cosmetics costs $26.35.
They are sold at a 33 1/3% profit.

Profit = $26.35 × 33 1/3% profit.

Selling Price = $26.35 + $8.78 or $35.13

Loss occurs when the selling price is less than cost.

Example: An order of cosmetics costs $26.35. They were sold at 33 1/3% loss or below cost.

Loss = $26.35 × 33 1/3% or $8.78

Selling Price = $26.35 − $8.78 or $17.57

Inventory

Inventory is an itemized list of merchandise, supplies or equipment on hand.

When taking inventory, the merchandise, supplies or equipment on hand are counted and recorded. This is done usually at the end of a business year, but sometimes more frequently. To obtain the cost of goods sold, the amount left on hand must be subtracted from the amount purchased. For example: $2000 was paid for supplies in one year. The inventory at the end of the year showed $400 worth on hand; therefore, $1600 was spent for supplies used.

Net Profit is the amount left after all expenses are paid.

Net profit equals the amount taken in minus operating expenses.

Operating expenses are all the costs of running the business such as salaries, rent, supplies used, telephone, power, heat, etc.

Depreciation

Depreciation is the decrease in the value of property or equipment through use, age, or becoming outmoded.

The depreciation of the equipment must be included in the operating expenses of the business. The equipment in a beauty salon will depreciate at least 10% each year, and at the end of 10 years it will be worthless or outmoded.

Problems

1. Miss Jones paid $68.85 for an order of cosmetics. She sold them all and received a 40% profit.

   a. How much did she receive for the cosmetics?
   b. How much was her gain?

   a. _____   b. _____

2. Mrs. Sears' income from services in her beauty salon for one month was $1530.65. .
   Her expenses were:

   Salaries: $985.00   Rent: $245.00
   Utilities: $49.73   Laundry: $51.42
   Supplies: $127.80   Miscellaneous Expenses: $12.70

   a. How much were her expenses?
   b. Did she gain or lose and how much?
   c. What was the percent gain or loss?

   a. _____   b. _____   c. _____

3. Miss Adams worked for 50 weeks in a year and received an average salary of $156.00 per week. The income from her services was $17,600.

   a. What is the difference between her salary and the income from services?
   b. Since it is estimated that every cosmetologist must double her salary, did her employer gain or lose, and how much?
   c. What is the approximate percent of gain or loss?

   a. _____   b. _____   c. _____

4. A beauty salon owner bought 8 new hairdryers at $247.50 each with a 20% discount. These dryers depreciated at the rate of 12% each year.

   a. How much did the owner pay for the dryers?
   b. What was the value of the dryers at the end of 5 years?
   c. What is the approximate percent of depreciation in the 5 years?

   a. _____   b. _____   c. _____

5. Miss Mead bought 20 gallons of shampoo at $11.25 per gallon. Through carelessness of the beauticians when shampooing, 20% of the shampoo was wasted.

   a. How much of the shampoo was wasted? _____

   b. How much did this waste cost Miss Mead? _____

49

6. A beauty salon owner bought 6 doz. bottles of cold wave lotion which cost $37.20 per dozen. One bottle is sufficient to give a complete cold wave. The employees were careless and wasted the amount equal to 1 bottle out of every 4.

   a. How many bottles were wasted out of the 6 dozen purchased? _____

   b. How much was the cost of the waste? _____

   c. What is the cost of each bottle of lotion? _____

7. A beauty salon charges $25.00 for one type of cold wave. The costs of giving the wave are: salary $12.00; permanent wave lotion $3.60; other expenses $6.25.

   a. What is the cost of each permanent wave? _____

   b. What percent profit is realized on the wave? _____

8. Miss Mead's expenses for one month were $2062.05. Her income was $2738.35.

   What percent profit did she make on the month's business? _____
   Note: Profit ÷ Cost = % Profit

9. Miss Mead took inventory of the cosmetics for resale on hand at the end of the fiscal year. The inventory showed cosmetics worth $189.65 retail, left unsold. Her profit from sales was $618.50.

   a. Find the amount of cosmetics sold. _____

   b. What is the cost of cosmetics unsold if they were marked for 33 1/3% profit? _____

INTEREST

Simple Interest is a service charge for the use of money.

It is figured on the amount of money borrowed at a given rate or percent for a stated length of time.

Interest = Principal × Rate × Time.

Amount = Interest + Principal.

Principal is the sum of money loaned or borrowed.

Interest is the sum of money paid for the use of the principal.

Rate of Interest is the part of 100 expressed as hundredths or as % paid for the use of $1.00 for 1 year.

One year is *Unit of Time* in interest calculation.

Interest is figured on the basis of 360 days per year.

Simple or Average Interest is figured on the basis of 30 days per month.

Promissory Note

A *Promissory Note* is a paper on which the borrower fills out and signs a written promise to pay back the amount of money borrowed. It may or may not carry interest.

If the lender expects interest the note will specify *with interest* at a given rate.

Example:

$300.00   New Rochelle, N.Y.   7/17/82

One   year
after   date   I   promise to pay to
the order of ___William Smith___
THREE HUNDRED AND NO/100----------------------------DOLLARS
Value received, with interest at 6%
Due July 17, 1983   John Doe

JOHN DOE is the *maker* of the note.

The lender, WILLIAM SMITH, is known as the *payee*.

The amount of $300 is called the *face* of the note.

July 17, 1983 is known as the *due date* or *date of maturity*.

Some states have a fixed rate called the *legal rate*.

Charging a higher rate is forbidden except in certain circumstances stated by the state law. The borrower and lender may agree on a lower rate.

Example:

Find the amount JOHN DOE must pay WILLIAM SMITH on July 17, 1983.

Interest = Principal × Rate × Time.
Interest = $300 × 6% × 1 yr. = $18.00.
Amount = Principal + Interest.
Amount = $300 + $18 = $318.

Cancellation Method

Find the interest on $100 at 6% for 1 year, 3 months and 10 days.

To find the interest for years, months and days, change all to days and use them as part of a year.

Example:

$$\begin{array}{ll} 1 \text{ year} & = 360 \text{ days} \\ 3 \text{ mos.} & = 90 \text{ days} \\ 10 \text{ days} & = \underline{10} \text{ days} \\ & 460 \text{ days} \end{array}$$

Base × Rate × Time

$$\$\cancel{100} \times \frac{\cancel{6}}{\cancel{100}} \times \frac{\cancel{460}}{\cancel{360}} = \frac{46}{6} \qquad \frac{46}{6} = \$7.666 \text{ or } \$7.67 \text{ interest}$$

Find interest on $500 at 2½% for 1½ years.

Example: Base × Rate × Time

$$\frac{250}{\cancel{500}} \times 5 \times \frac{\cancel{540}}{\cancel{360}} = \$18.75 \text{ Interest}$$
$$ \underset{\cancel{2}}{} \underset{\cancel{360}}{}$$

60 DAY METHOD
at 6%

Many loans are made for short periods of time in which case the 60 day method at 6% is used for convenience. To find the interest of any amount of money at 6% for 60 days, move the decimal point TWO places to the left.

Example: $500 at 6% for 60 days.

Move decimal 2 places = $5.00

To find interest for 90 days, first find interest for 60 days and for 30 days (1/2 the amount for 60) and add.

Example: $500 at 6% for 90 days.

Interest 60 days = $5.00
Interest 30 days =   2.50

$5.00 + $2.50 = $7.50 Interest.

Exercise XXX

Using the 6% - 60 day method, find the interest of:

1.

$420 for 60 days = _____

2.

$150 for 60 days = _____

3.

$500 for 12 days = _____

4.

$300 for 6 days = _____

5.

$80 for 15 days = _____

6.

$250 for 66 days = _____

7.

$475 for 42 days = _____

8.

$900 for 78 days = _____

9.

$6000 for 90 days = _____

10.

$960 for 80 days = _____

How To Find Interest By The 6% Method With Other Rates of Interest

Example: Find interest on $500 at 4% for 80 days.

$500 @ 6% for 60 days = $5.00
80 days − 60 days = 20 days
20 days = 1/3 of 60 days
1/3 of $5.00 = $1.666
$5.00 + $1.666 = $6.666

2 222
4% is 2/3 of 6%. 2/3 × $6.666 = $4.44 Interest

Exercise XXXI

Using the 6% method find the interest of the following:

1.

$720 at 5% for 75 days = _____

2.

$120 at 7% for 60 days = _____

3.

$840 at 8% for 88 days = _____

4.

$450 at 5% for 40 days = _____

5.

$3600 at 5% for 48 days = _____

6.

$660 at 3% for 28 days = _____

7.

$1500 at 7% for 44 days = _____

8.

$425 at 2% for 72 days = _____

9.

$6600 at 4% for 96 days = ___

10.

$5400 at 2 1/2% for 70 days − _____

Problems

1. Mrs. James borrowed $650 from the bank to make a down payment on some new equipment. She repaid the loan 4 months later with interest at 6%.

   Find the total amount she paid the bank. _____

2. Miss Mead borrowed $2200 from the bank to remodel her beauty salon. The loan was for 1 year at 12%, the interest to be paid in advance and deducted from the amount of the loan.
   a. How much was the interest? _____
   b. How much cash did she actually receive? _____

3. Mrs. Jenkins arranged for a 90 day loan of $1500 at her bank in order to buy the building in which her beauty salon was located. She signed and endorsed a note payable to her order. She was then credited with the proceeds after a discount of 12% per annum was deducted.
   a. What was the amount credited to her account? _____

4. Miss Adams deposited $400 in the bank which pays 5% interest. She withdrew the money from the bank at the end of 2 years.

   How much did she withdraw? _____

   Note: Compound Interest means that the interest is added to the principal, thus making a new principal for the next interest period.

5. Miss Brown bought 7 bonds for $50 each on which she was paid 11% interest compounded semi-annually. She sold them at the end of 3 years.
   a. How much did she receive for them?
   b. How much did her investment earn?

   a. _____   b. _____

6. On February 1, Mrs. Jones borrowed $750 from the finance corporation at 16% interest to enable her to carry on the business in her beauty salon. Business improved and she was able to repay the loan with interest on July 1, same year.

   How much did she pay? _____

7. In order to take advantage of a 2% discount for cash on a shipment of beauty equipment, Mrs. James borrowed $1200 for 24 days at 6%.
   a. How much interest did she have to pay?
   b. How much did she save?

   a. _____   b. _____

8. Mrs. Jones made a personal loan to her partner of $1500 on November 5, at 8% interest. The loan was repaid on January 10th.

   What was the amount of interest paid on the loan? _____

9. What is the interest on $975 at 9% for 3 years, 2 months and 15 days? _____

INSTALLMENT BUYING

Installment Buying means the article is paid for in a stated number of payments. A down payment is made and the balance in installments.

The buyer does not acquire legal ownership of the goods until the last payment is made. The seller has special expenses such as investigation of the buyer's credit, bookkeeping, money paid for the article and collection. He must, therefore, charge a higher price than for a cash sale.

The rate of interest is usually very high on installment buying. Much money is saved by paying cash if at all possible.

Example:

Two used hair dryers cost $280.00 cash. They may be purchased by paying $28.00 and the balance in 18 monthly payments of $16.10 each. Find the difference between cash and installment buying. Find the percent paid on time.

18 payments @ $16.10 = $289.80 plus $28.00 down payment = $317.80

Cash price $280.00. Installment payment is $37.80 paid over cash price.

$$\begin{array}{r} .135 \\ \hline 280\overline{)37.800} \\ 28\ 0 \\ \hline 9\ 80 \\ 8\ 40 \\ \hline 1\ 400 \\ 1\ 400 \end{array} \qquad = \qquad 13\tfrac{1}{2}\% \text{ finance charge}$$

Problems

1. A beauty salon owner wanted to buy a piece of equipment priced at $720 cash or $180 cash and 12 monthly installments at $49.00 each. She did not have the money for cash payment.

    a) How much could be saved by borrowing $720 at 6% interest for the 12 months?

    b. What is the rate of interest on the installment buying?

    a. _____   b. _____

2. A beauty salon owner buys a rug for her reception room. The price is $630. This is to be paid for in 8 monthly payments after the initial down payment of 1/3 of the price is made.

    What is the amount of each monthly payment? _____

3. Miss Mead installed an air conditioner in her beauty salon, the price of which was $875. She paid $75 cash when she signed the contract.

    When the conditioner was installed she paid 25% of the balance in cash. Interest on the balance at 12% for 1 1/2 years was added to the amount unpaid. This was to be paid off in six equal quarterly installments.

    a. What was the amount of each installment?
    b. What was the total cost?

    a. _____   b. _____

4. Mrs. Young bought some badly needed equipment for $1240. She was unable to pay cash. She bought it on the installment plan and paid $200 as a down payment. She paid the balance in 13 installments of $105 each.

    a. How much more than the cash price did she pay?
    b. Approximately what percent interest did she pay?

a. _____   b. _____

5. A cosmetologist bought a watch paying $7.50 down and $1.25 per week for 50 weeks. The cash price was $60.

    a. How much would she have saved by paying cash?
    b. What percent in excess of the cash price was the time payment plan?

a. _____   b. _____

6. Miss Hammond bought a reconditioned hairdryer for $140.00 The dealer allowed her $30.00 on her old dryer which he took. She made a cash down payment of $10.00 and agreed to pay the balance at $12.50 per week for 10 weeks.

    a. How much would have been her saving on the cash deal?
    b. What percent carrying charge did she pay?

a. _____   b. _____

7. A beauty salon owner bought a television set for her beauty salon for $486 plus 6% sales tax. She paid 33 1/3% of the total as a down payment. The dealer added a 5% finance fee on the balance. She paid the balance in 50 equal installments. How much was each payment?

                _____

8. Mrs. James needed a better car for transportation to her beauty salon. She was allowed $425 trade-in on her old car towards the one priced at $3420.00 She paid $667 cash besides the allowance for her car and the balance in 12 equal monthly installments. What were her monthly payments?

                _____

9. Miss Mead bought a scalp steamer. She paid $25 cash and $9 per month for one year.

    a. What is the installment price?
    b. What is the cash price if 9% discount is allowed from the installment price?

a. _____   b. _____

SALARY AND COMMISSIONS

Salary is money paid to an employee for the services he/she has rendered his/her employer.

Commission is a percentage paid on the price of an article or for services rendered.

Earnings

Cosmetologists are usually paid by one of three methods: *straight salary, salary and commission* or *commission only.*

In most states there is a minimum salary scale for cosmetologists.

Straight salary means the cosmetologist is paid by salary only. The amount depends on the locality, amount of business and the individual's ability.

Salary and Commission means the cosmetologist is guaranteed a salary and is also paid a commission on the beauty services performed.

The amount of salary and commission is subject to agreement between employer and employee. Usually the commission is paid on the amount of money taken in from services after the guaranteed salary has been doubled. It is estimated that a cosmetologist must double her salary before the employer realizes any profit on services. Sometimes a lower commission is paid on money taken in from services over and above the guaranteed salary.

Expenses such as rent, heat, utilities, interest on investment, depreciation, insurance and other incidentals amount to approximately as much as the cosmetologist's salary.

Commission only means the cosmetologist is paid a commission or percent on all the money taken in from his services.

The commission rarely amounts to more than 50%.

Taxes

Both the employer and the employee must pay taxes, such as *Federal Social Security* and *Federal Income Tax.* Some states have also a *State Income Tax.* There are cities that charge *Income Tax* as well. Thus taxes are paid on the cosmetologist's salary. The cosmetologist does not receive his full salary because of these deductions. These are also added expenses for the employer.

Federal Social Security is a tax on an employee's salary to help meet the cost of old age benefits to which the employee will be entitled upon reaching the retirement age.

Federal Income Tax is a government tax on salary, with deductions allowed for dependents, charities, medical expenses, etc. The government furnishes a "Wage Bracket Table" which enables an employer to determine the deduction quickly.

Problems

1. Miss Adams is paid a straight salary of $156.00 a week plus a 10% commission on all cosmetics sales. She sold $61.10 worth of cosmetics in one week. The income for her services amounted to $275.25. She had a tax deduction of $28.72.
   a) How much did she actually receive?
   b) How much profit did Miss Adams' employer realize on her services above double her salary?

   a) _____ b) _____

2. Miss Brown is paid $153.00 per week plus 40% on all money she earns in excess of $153. Her services amounted to $291.75. Her cosmetics sales amounted to $37, on which she received 15% commission. Her withholding tax amounted to $41.42.
   a) How much commission did she receive on both services and sales?
   b) What is the total net salary she received?

   a) _____ b) _____

3. Miss Jones is paid on the commission basis only. She is paid 50% on all money taken in from her services. She also receives 15% commission on all cosmetic sales. One week her services amounted to $298.75 and her sales amounted to $73.40. Her withholding tax amounted to $27.26. How much salary did she actually receive?

   _____

4. Mr. James' service slips for one week were as follows: Tues. $160.25, Wed. $187.00, Thurs. $183.50, Fri. $205.00, Sat. $225.50. His salary is $165.00 per week and 50% commission on all over double his salary. He pays 7% of his total salary for Social Security. His withholding tax is $79.80. What is his "take-home" pay?

   _____

5. Miss Arnold's service slips totaled $280.50 for the week. She sold cosmetics amounting to $55.65 on which she received 15% commission. She received a straight salary of $153.00 per week. Her withholding tax amounted to $22.70 because she has one dependent. Social Security tax is 7% of her total salary.
   a) What was her "take-home" pay?
   b) How much more than her weekly salary did she earn for her employer?

   a) _____ b) _____

6. A cosmetologist's service slips for one week were as follows: Tues. $75.35, Wed. $83.60, Thurs. $112.40, Fri. $105.00, Sat. $118.80. She receives a salary of $156.00 per week and 50% commission on all over double her salary. Her cosmetic sales on which she received 10% commission amounted to $44.30. She has two dependents so her withholding tax was $36.70. Social Security amounts to 7% of salary before deductions.

   a) How much money did she take in for the week?

   b) What is the total deduction from her salary for the week?

   c) What is her "take-home" pay?

   a) _____   b) _____   c) _____

7. A cosmetologist earns $381.00 in services for the week. Her sales of cosmetics amounts to $46.25 on which she receives 15%. Her salary amounts to 50% of her earnings from services. Her withholding tax amounts to $31.20 and Social Security is 7% of salary plus sales commissions.

   a) How much does she receive from services and sales?

   b) What is her "take-home" pay?

   a) _____   b) _____

8. Miss Scott's average income from services was $92.00 per day for five working days. She receives a salary of $149.00 and a 40% commission on sales exceeding double her income. Her withholding tax is $20.00 and Social Security is 7% of total pay.

   a) What is her total income for services?

   b) What is the total amount of sales on which she receives a 40% commission?

   c) What is her "take-home" pay?

   a) _____   b) _____   c) _____

9. A beauty supply salesman receives a commission of 8% on sales of equipment and 14½% on supplies. His sales for a three month period amounted to $49,675 for equipment and $3865 for supplies. His withholding tax amounted to $52.40 per week and Social Security 7% of weekly salary.

   a) What were the earnings for the three-month period?

   b) How much did he average per month?

   c) How much was his weekly "take-home" pay?

   a) _____   b) _____   c) _____

CASH ACCOUNT

In order to conduct a business successfully the owner must keep a record of all income and all expenditures. This is necessary to show the amount of profit or loss at the end of the year. It is needed also to compute the government taxes that must be paid on the profit.

If the business does not show a substantial profit, it cannot continue to operate for any period of time. The profit is the owner's compensation for money invested in the business, and also for the work and responsibility of keeping the business going.

This brief introduction of keeping a cash record will help the student to better understand the Bookkeeping for Cosmetology which definitely should follow this Mathematics Course.

Financial Records

Assets are things that a person owns.
Liabilities are the debts the person owes.
Creditor is the one to whom the debt is owed.
Total liabilities are the amounts owed to all creditors.
Personal liabilities are debts of an individual for his personal affairs.
Business liabilities are debts incurred in the operation of his business.
Proprietorship means ownership or the difference between assets and his liabilities.
Capital is another term sometimes given to proprietorship.

There are two sides to the record when recording a cash account, the *debit* (dr.) side, and opposite, the *credit* (cr.) side. All cash on hand and cash received are recorded in the left-hand column called the debit side of the cash account. All cash paid out is recorded in the right-hand column called the credit side of the cash account.

Balance of Cash on Hand is the difference between the debit and credit of the account, providing the debit side is the larger amount.

In *Closing the Account* the balance is entered on the lesser side to make the total of that side equal to the total of the larger side of the account. The account is closed by ruling, as illustrated, showing the two equal totals.

Example:

CASH

(Dr.) Debit						(Cr.) Credit		
19								
March	1	Balance	3584	72	March	1	Rent	400	00
	6	Services	664	75			Salaries	180	35
	6	Mdse.	156	90		12	Salaries	140	89
	12	Services	600	75		12	Ace. Co. Supp.	200	00
	12	Mdse.	130	05		12	Light and Telephone	120	73
			5137	17				1041	97
		Balance	4095	20			Balance	4095	20
								5137	17

60

Problems

Rule a form of cash account. Write a cash account for the following transactions.

1. Balance as of Sept. 1, $1300; Sept. 1, Received in services $130.25, Mdse. $13.40; Paid Ace Supply Co. Supplies $123.60.
    Sept. 2, Received in Services $141.75; Sept. 4, Received in services $188.90, Mdse. $12.40; Paid out, telephone $19.48; Sept. 5, Received in Services $171.20, Mdse. $14.30;Paid out rent $295.

    Dr.   Cr.   Bal.

2. Write a cash account for Miss Smith's business for the year January 1 to December 31.
    Balance $1760.84; Income from Services $7151.90, Mdse. $1031., Cost of Mdse. and Supplies $2183.72; Paid out for rent $1040, Electricity $195.62, Gas $50.60, Telephone $108.40, Laundry $107.12, Taxes and License Fees $71.42, Miscellaneous Expenses $112.59.

    Dr.   Cr.   Bal.

3. Business for one week: Cash on Hand $1202.23; Income from services $1841.75; Cosmetic Sales $180.05; Paid out: Postage $12.50, Cleaning Floors $30.00, Laundry $27.48, Supplies $210.00, Salaries $378.89.

    Dr.   Cr.   Bal.

4. Business for one week: Cash on Hand $1308.51; Income from services $1586.50; Cosmetic Sales $154.75. Expenses: Charity $26.00, Insurance $160.00, Laundry $28.89, Salary $163.76, Salary $174.69.

    Dr.   Cr.   Bal.

5. Using the balance from Problem #4, write out a cash account for the following: Income from Services $1701.25, Cosmetic Sales $132.40. Expenses: May 7, Plumbing $42.75, Supplies $140.00, Cleaning $19.50; May 8, Supplies $85.00, Magazines $15.00; May 9, Laundry $30.14; May 10, Taxes $79.20; May 11, Salary $171.31, Salary $183.84, Salary $153.00.

    Dr.   Cr.   Bal.

6. Cash on hand $1433.79; May 1, Income from Services $192.50, Sales $17.20. Paid: Rent $295.00, Supplies $123.40. May 2, Income from Services $152.50, Sales $15.10. Paid: Express $2.38, Electrician $18.50, Supplies $79.60. May 3, Income from Services $210.75, Sales $19.00. Paid Advertising $52.00. May 4, Income from Services $167.75, Sales $18.60. Paid: Electricity $76.29, Telephone $51.27. May 5, Income from Services $193.75, Sales $14.20. Paid out salary $142.03, Salary $154.30, Salary $139.00.

   Dr.   Cr.   Bal.

7. Cash on hand $1365.00; Income from services for one week $1228.40, Sales $58.60. Paid for supplies $188.45, New equipment $115.00, Salary $129.81, Salary $118.20, Laundry $18.12.

   Dr.   Cr.   Bal.

8. Cash on hand $245.65; Income from services $599.60, Sales from cosmetics $39.78. Paid: Rent $175.00, Electricity $42.42, Gas $6.33, Supplies $88.20, Salary $105.00, Salary $112.00.

   Dr.   Cr.   Bal.

9. Mrs. Jones started the week with $676.80 cash on hand. Her business for the week was as follows: Tues., Income from Services $82.60, Cosmetic Sales $36.30, Paid out supplies $52.00; Wed., Services $81.10, Cosmetic Sales $16.95, Paid out Laundry $21.04, Window Washing $18.00; Thurs., Services $135.15, Mdse. $23.05, Paid out Rent $260.00, Payment on Equipment $65.00; Fri., Services $130.30, Mdse. $34.08, Paid out Telephone $30.40, Electricity $46.25; Sat., Services $141.80, Mdse. $39.15, Paid out Salary $139.00, Salary $156.00.

   Dr.   Cr.   Bal.

BANK ACCOUNTS —— CHECKS

Practically every business concern and many individuals have bank checking accounts. A checking account is a great convenience in making payments of bills. A check instead of cash may be given in payment for a bill.

Paying by check is safer than keeping a large sum of money on hand to pay bills. A check may be sent through the mails with comparative safety, while sending cash would incur a great risk or loss.

Before a person can write a check, he must first deposit a sum of money in the bank in his *checking account.* Care must be taken not to write checks amounting to more than the cash deposited. A cancelled check is a receipt for payment of a bill.

Opening a Bank Account

To open a bank account, a person must sign a signature card, with address, employment, etc. A depositor should always sign his checks with the same style of signature he used on his signature card. If there is a difference in style of signature, the bank might refuse to pay out the depositor's money on suspicion of forgery.

SIGNATURE CARD: Example

Deposit Slip

A deposit slip must be made with the same signature as on the signature card, noting date, cash (silver and bills) and checks. The bank gives the depositor checkbooks. These books come in either small folding form for the pocket or larger book form for desk or office use. He is also given a bankbook which shows a record of all deposits made.

DEPOSIT SLIP: Example

Checks

The checkbook has a stub on the left of the check on which the depositor keeps a record of his checking account. The balance of the account is at the top, with deposits and amounts of each check recorded on each stub as they are made. The party to whom the check is made is also listed, as well as for what it is in payment.

No.			
		19	
To			
For			
Balance brought forward			
Amount deposited			
Amount deposited			
Total Credits			
Amt. this check			
Check chg.		10	
Other chgs.			
LESS: Total charges			

No.＿＿＿＿＿＿   **1-2**
                  210

＿＿＿＿＿＿＿＿ 19 ＿＿

Pay to the
order of ＿＿＿＿＿＿＿＿＿＿＿＿＿＿＿＿＿＿＿＿＿ $＿＿＿＿＿

＿＿＿＿＿＿＿＿＿＿＿＿＿＿＿＿＿＿＿＿＿＿＿＿＿＿＿＿ Dollars

THE CHASE MANHATTAN BANK
NATIONAL ASSOCIATION
220TH ST. AND WHITE PLAINS RD.
BRONX, N.Y. 10467

⑆0 ⑈10 ⑈000 ⑆: 0⑆ ⑈0⑈0⑈0⑈0⑈⑆

The *drawer* of a check is the person who writes the check.

The *drawee* of a check is the bank on which the check is drawn.

The *payee* is the person or concern to whom the check is made payable.

Before the bank will accept a check for deposit, the payee must *endorse* it by writing his name across the back of the left-hand end of the check.

ENDORSEMENT OF A CHECK

There are three types of endorsements. A *blank* endorsement makes the check payable to anyone who may have it in his possession.

Example

John Jones

A *full endorsement* makes the check payable to a particular person. This person must endorse it before he can collect on it.

Example:

Pay to the order of
John Jones

A *restrictive endorsement* limits or restricts the use of the check to a particular purpose.

Example:

For Deposit

Bank Statement

Periodically, or upon request, the bank furnishes a *statement* of the depositor's account. This shows the balance brought forward from previous statement, the deposits made, the checks drawn and presented to the bank for payment, and the balance or money remaining in the account.

Sometimes, some of the checks drawn have not been presented for payment by the time the statement is made. The bank sends all the checks on which payments have been made along with the statement. By comparing the statement with the checkbook stubs, it can be readily seen what checks have not been returned to the bank for payment. To get the checkbook balance to agree with the bank statement, it is necessary to subtract the sum of the outstanding checks from the checkbook balance. This is called *reconciling the bank balance.*

Example:

Bank Statement Balance $1365.38
Checks outstanding:

#103 ------ $ 63.45	
#105 ------ 75.40	
#108 ------ 103.36	242.21

Adjusted balance $1123.17

Problems

1. Reconcile the bank balance of the following:
   Bank Statement Balance...$1021.84
   Checks Outstanding:
# 50	4.00
# 51	14.82
# 54	6.20
# 58	200.00

   _____

2. Reconcile the bank balance of the following:
   Previous Bank Statement Balance, $1603.41; Checks Drawn: #30—$6.85;
   #31—$14.13; #32—$25.25; Deposited, $55.65; Checks Drawn: #33—$46.82;
   #34—$207.87; #35—$89.69; Checks #31, #33, #35 are still outstanding.

   _____

3. Miss Adams' check stub balance on May 5th was $161.42. That week she drew the
   following checks: #20 for $18.75; #25 for $4.82; #26 for $12.34. The following
   week she deposited $35.00 and drew the following checks: #27 for $10.85; #28 for
   $21.40. She received a bank statement showing a balance of $140.60.

   Which check had not been cashed? _____

4. Miss Brown opened a special checking account. The bank charges 5¢ service
   charge for each deposit and for each check drawn. She makes the following
   deposits and writes the checks: March 3, Deposit $175; Checks #1 for $3.25; #2 for
   $10.89; #3 for $23.40. March 10, Deposit $66.30; Checks #4 for $27.08; #5 for
   $35.00.

   What is the balance at the end of the above transaction? _____

5. Mrs. Jones opened a regular checking account with a deposit of $450. She made
   the following deposits during the month:
   $350.40, $293.23, $328.47, $262.80. Her checks amounted to $1263.20. The bank
   charged $6.00 to her account in payment for a safe deposit box rental.

   What was her checkbook balance at the end of the month? _____

6. Rule and fill out 3 signature cards to be used when opening a checking account.

7. Rule and fill out 3 deposit slips similar to the illustration shown.

8. Rule and fill out three checks and stubs similar to the illustration shown.

9. Endorse the three checks in #8 with one blank endorsement, one full
   endorsement, and one restrictive endorsement.

10. Make up a problem in reconciling a bank balance for the rest of the class to solve.

INSURANCE

Insurance is a written agreement by an insurance company to pay for losses or damages according to the conditions stated in the agreement.

Insurance Terms

The Policy is the written contract or agreement.

Face of the Policy is the amount of money to be paid in case of losses or damages.

Premiums are payments made by the insured party for the protection against losses and damages.

The amount of each premium varies with the type of insurance and the amount of risk taken. The greater the risk the more the insured party must pay. Premiums are paid at regular intervals as specified in the policy.

Insurance companies invest the money paid in by the insured persons from which they receive interest, thereby accumulating a surplus with which to pay for losses by the insured. In many instances, an insured person will pay premiums on a policy indefinitely and never have a loss, as in the case of fire insurance. She is paying for protection just in case she should be unfortunate and lose all her possessions due to a fire.

Policy Holder is the party insured.

The Term of the policy is the length of time the policy is in force.

Kinds of Insurance

There are many kinds of insurance. The cosmetologist should be familiar with the important ones for her own protection, such as life insurance, personal insurance, property insurance, automobile insurance and theft insurance.

Life Insurance is a form of insurance that pays the stated amount of money in case of accident, sickness or death.

Property insurance covers the insured person in case of damage to the property of others.

Fire Insurance is an insurance whereby the company pays the policyholder for losses caused by accidental fires. The face of the policy is rarely ever more than 80% of the value of the property.

Liability Insurance covers the costs of the policyholder for injury to others caused by her actions, automobile, a fallen tree and other accidents.

Automobile Insurance is a form of liability insurance and covers damage to property of others and for personal injury.

Collision Insurance is another form of automobile insurance which covers costs of damages to one's own car.

Fire Insurance

Example:

Miss Mead owns the building in which her beauty salon is located. She has it insured for $50,000. She pays $2.67 per hundred for the insurance. Find the amount of the premium she pays per year.

$50,000 ÷ 100 = 500

$2.67 × 500 = $1335 premium per year.

An insurance policy may be cancelled by either the company or the insured party before the policy expires. In that event the unearned premium will be returned to the insured. If a policy is written for less than a year, the company charges what is known as the *short-rate scale*. This is a certain percent of the yearly premium for the month or months covered.

Example:

$15,000 ÷ 100 = 150   100% − 40% = 60%

150 × +1.00 = $150   60% of 150 = $90.00

Problems

1. A business block in which a beauty salon was located was insured for $90,000. The yearly premium was $2.20 per $100.

   Find the yearly premium. _____

2. Miss Mead insured the equipment in her beauty salon for $12,000 at the rate of 5½% for 2 years.

   Find the amount of the premium per year. _____

3. A cosmetologist insures her home for $28,500 for a period of 3 years at the rate of $1.75 per $100.

   Find the premium for one year. _____

4. Mrs. Jones' beauty salon was insured for $22,000 and the merchandise for $1850. The insurance per year on the beauty salon was $1.97 per $100 and $1.95 per $100 on the merchandise.

   Find the premium paid. _____

5. Miss Jones' car was insured against fire for $2800 at 2¾% rate for one year.

   How much was the premium? _____

6. The owner of the business building in which Mrs. Leons' beauty salon was located paid a premium of $2062.50. The rate of insurance was 3½%.

   For how much was the building insured?

   $B = \dfrac{P}{R}$ _____

7. Miss Brown insured the equipment in her beauty salon. She paid $962.50 which was at the rate of 5½% of the face of the policy.

   What was the face of the policy or for how much was the equipment insured? _____

8. The owner of a beauty salon had it insured for $19,000. The total value of the property is $22,000. If he should have a fire and the loss amounted to $6000, how much insurance can he collect? _____

9. A beautician paid $8500 for a new car. After one year the second hand value was 80% of the list price. The fire insurance company insured the car for 70% of the second hand value

   How much was the face of the policy on the car? _____

NOTE:

   Problems on the other insurance will not be given here because of the limited time that can be devoted to this course. Also, some of them need reference tables to solve the problems; while others are too complicated to be included.

TEST # 1

1. *Addition:* Copy 47865 --- 1st row
   Add 93276 --- 2nd row

   Below 2nd row write the sum of row 1 and 2
          3rd row write the sum of row 2 and 3
          4th row write the sum of row 3 and 4

   Continue until you have 8 rows. Draw a line and add the entire column. Label the sum.

2. *Subtraction:*

a	b	c
93.203	7749	37,451
−30.866	−4152	−35,689

d	e
975,312,468	1607.5362
−286,987,539	−1098.7496

Label the subtrahend in #e.
Label the minuend in #e.

3. *Multiplication:*

a	b	c
667	9284	8638
× 557	× 8759	× 6387

d	e
7596	9986
× 7518	× 8638

Label the multiplicand in #e.
Label the multiplier in #e.
Label the product in #e.

4. *Division:*

a

$252{,}576 \div 72 = $ _____

b

$855{,}172 \div 487 = $ _____

c

$691{,}642 \div 389 = $ _____

d

$760{,}025 \div 81 = $ _____

e

$348{,}409 \div 24 = $ _____

In #e label the dividend, the divisor, the quotient and the remainder.

5. a. Give an example of a proper fraction.
   b. Give an example of an improper fraction.
   c. Give an example of a mixed number.
   d. Label the numerator and the denominator in the fraction 5/6.
   e. Show how to reduce the fraction 9/15 to its lowest terms.
   f. Show how to reduce the fraction 4/5 to higher terms.
   g. Show how the mixed number 4 2/3 can be reduced to a fraction.
   h. Show what must be done to the fractions 3/4 and 2/3 before they can be added or subtracted.

a. _____   e. _____

b. _____   f. _____

c. _____   g. _____

d. _____   h. _____

TEST # 2

1. *Addition of Fractions:*

   a

   1/4 + 1/5 + 1/10 = _____

   b

   2/9 + 5/12 + 2/3 = _____

   c

   1/3 + 3/4 + 3/8 = _____

   d

   3/8 + 1/5 + 3/4 = _____

   e

   7 1/2 + 2 1/3 = _____

2. *Subtraction of Fractions:*

   a

   9/10 − 2/3 = _____

   b

   5/12 − 1/8 = _____

   c

   16 3/4 − 14 1/3 = _____

   d

   5/6 − 2/3 − 5/12 = _____

   e

   5 1/2 − 3 2/3 = _____

3. *Multiplication of Fractions:*

   a

   5 × 2/3 = _____

   b

   11/24 × 4/33 = _____

   c

   5/9 × 9/10 × 11/12 × 6/7 = _____

   d

   28 1/4 × 4/7 × 7/8 = _____

   e

   2 1/4 × 1 3/5 × 3 7/8 × 5/63 = _____

4. *Division of Fractions:*

a

$3/5 \div 3/10 =$ _____

b

$8/25 \div 36/45 =$ _____

c

$12\ 1/2 \div 5/14 =$ _____

d

$1/4 \div 1/3 + 5/4 - 3/2 + 1/4 =$ _____

e

$3/6 \times 1/12 + 1/8 + 4/6 - 3/8 =$ _____

5. *Decimals:*

a. Change the following to decimals:
4/10, 35/100, 125/1000, 7/1000, 16/10000.

_____ _____ _____ _____ _____

b. Add: $6.57 + 2.0256 + .0568 + 18.0446 =$ _____

c. Subtract: 84.635 from 792.57 = _____

d. Multiply: $73.26 \times .624 =$ _____

e. Divide: .03125 by 125 = _____

TEST # 3

1. *Percent:*

   a

   45% of 20 = _____

   b

   200% of 82 = _____

   c

   17% of 120 = _____

   d

   79% of 500 = _____

   e

   1 3/4% of 60 = _____

2. *Change to percentage:*

   a

   18/100 = _____%

   b

   7/8 = _____%

   c

   .08 = _____%

   d

   .83 1/3 = _____%

   e

   .0625 = _____%

3. *What percent of:*

   a

   384 is 64 = _____%

   b

   .125 is .05 = _____%

   c

   97 is 6.79 _____%

   d

   82 is 143.5 = _____%

   e

   1296 is 810 = _____%

4. *Find the base:*

   a
   40 is 12 1/2% = _____

   b
   360 is 40% = _____

   c
   97.2 is 12% = _____

   d
   108 is 6 1/4% = _____

   e
   96 is 44 4/9% = _____

5. *Find the selling price:*

   a. $160 discounts 25% and 10% = _____

   b. $420 discounts 40% and 16 2/3% = _____

   c. $12 discounts 20%, 10%, and 2% = _____

   d. $225.15 discounts 33 1/3% and 20% = _____

   e. $50 discounts 40% and 25% = _____

WEIGHTS AND MEASURES

Linear Measure

12 inches . . . . 1 foot (ft.)
 3 feet . . . . 1 yard (yd.)
5 1/2 yards . . . . 1 rod (rd.)
320 rods or 5,280 ft . . . . 1 mile (mi.)

Square Measure

144 square inches . . . . 1 square foot (sq. ft.)
9 square feet . . . . 1 square yd. (sq. yd.)
30½ square yards . . . . 1 square rod (sq. rd.)
160 square rods . . . . 1 acre (A)
640 acres . . . . 1 square mile (sq. mi.)

Liquid Measure

4 gills (gi.) . . . . 1 pint (pt.)
2 pints . . . . 1 quart (qt.)
4 quarts . . . . 1 gallon (gal.)
1 pint . . . . 16 ounces (oz.)
1 quart . . . . 32 ounces
1 gallon . . . . 128 ounces

Avoirdupois Weight

27 11/32 grains . . . . 1 dram (dr.)
16 drams . . . . 1 ounce (oz.)
16 ounces . . . . 1 pound (lb.)
100 pounds . . . . 1 hundred weight (cwt.)

Measure of Angles

60 seconds (") . . . . 1 minute (')
60 minutes . . . . 1 degree (°)
90 degrees . . . . 1 right angle
360 degrees . . . . 1 circle

COMMON UNITS

12 units	....	1 dozen (doz.)
12 dozen	....	1 gross (gr.)
144 units	....	1 gross
12 gross	....	1 great gross
20 units	....	1 score

PAPER MEASURE

24 sheets	....	1 quire
20 quires	....	1 ream (480 sheets)
500 sheets	....	1 Commercial Ream
2 reams	....	1 bundle
5 bundles	....	1 bale

TIME MEASURE

60 seconds	....	1 minute (min.)
60 minutes	....	1 hour (hr.)
24 hours	....	1 day (da.)
7 days	....	1 week (wk.)
4 weeks	....	1 month (mo.)
12 months	....	1 year (yr.)
52 weeks	....	1 year
365 days	....	1 common year
366 days	....	1 Leap year
10 years	....	1 decade
20 years	....	1 score
100 years	....	1 century

KITCHEN WEIGHTS AND MEASURES

4 large tablespoonfuls	....	1/2 gill
1 glass (ordinary tumbler)	....	1/2 pint
2 cups	....	1 pint
2 pints	....	1 quart
1 tablespoonful	....	1/2 ounce
1 wine glass (large)	....	2 ounces
16 tablespoonfuls	....	1 cup
60 drops	....	1 teaspoonful
3 teaspoonfuls	....	1 tablespoonful
4 tablespoonfuls	....	1/4 cup
1 tablespoonful	....	1/2 fluid ounce
1 ordinary cup	....	2 gills

A gallon of water (U.S. Standard) weighs 8 1/3 pounds and contains 231 cubic inches.

Steam rising from water at its boiling point (212 degrees) has a pressure equal to the atmosphere (14.7 pounds to the square inch at sea level).

ROMAN NUMERALS

I 1			XI 11	
II 2			XII 12	
III 3			XIII 13	
IV 4			XIV 14	
V 5			XV 15	
VI 6			XVI 16	
VII 7			XVII 17	
VIII 8			XVIII 18	
IX 9			XIX 19	
X 10			XX 20	

XXX 30	CCCC 400
XL 40	or
L 50	CD 400
LX 60	D 500
LXX 70	DC 600
LXXX 80	DCC 700
or	DCCC 800
XXC 80	CM 900
XC 90	M 1000
C 100	or
CC 200	CIC 1000
CCC 300	MM 2000

A dash line over and under a numeral multiplies the value by 1000.

Example: $\overline{X} = 10,000$ $\overline{L} = 50,000$

METRIC CONVERSION TABLE

SQUARE MEASURE

1 sq. inch =6.4516 sq. centimeters
1 sq. foot =9.29034 sq. decimeters
1 sq. yard = .836131 sq. meter
1 acre   = .40469 hectare
1 sq. mile =2.59 sq. kilometers

CUBIC MEASURE

1 cu. inch =16.3872 cu. centimeters
1 cu. foot = .028317 cu. meter
1 cu. yard = .76456 cu. meter

AVOIRDUPOIS MEASURE

1 ounce   =28.349527 grams
1 pound   = .453592 kilogram
1 short ton = .90718486 metric ton
1 long ton = 1.01604704 metric tons

LONG MEASURE

1 inch   =2.54 centimeters
1 yard   = .914401 meter
1 mile   =1.609347 kilometers

LIQUID MEASURE

1 pint   = .473167 liter
1 quart   = .946332 liter
1 gallon   =3.785329 liters

DRY MEASURE

1 pint   = .550599 liter
1 quart   =1.101197 liters
1 peck   =8.80958 liters
1 bushel   = .35238 hectoliter

7623